Paneer Bonanza

Enjoy cooking paneer in 55 wonderful ways

Prabhjot Mundhir

Publishers
UNICORN BOOKS

J-3/16 , Daryaganj, New Delhi-110002
☎ 23276539, 23272783, 23272784 • *Fax:* 011-23260518
E-mail: unicornbooks@vsnl.com
Website: www.unicornbooks.in

Distributors
Pustak Mahal, Delhi
E-mail: info@pustakmahal.com • *Website:* www.pustakmahal.com

Branches
Bangalore, Mumbai, Patna, Hyderabad

ISBN 978-81-7806-098-9

Edition : 2008

Printed at : Param Offsetters, Okhla, New Delhi-110020

Preface

Foods of the gods: Aryans called themselves gods or *devas* and the foods and drinks consumed by them are known as the *foods of gods*. What they actually used to eat between 1500 and 350 BC has been very well documented by **Rigveda.** Since the Aryan civilization was essentially an agricultural one, the cattle were an integral part of their life and milk and milk products were one of the most important food items. Milk products were used in various forms along with meats, grains, seeds, vegetables, fruits and nuts. *Paneer* was known as *Dadhanwat* and whey too was popularly used as a refreshing drink. That means ***Paneer* has an ancient heritage and it is traditional for Indians to consume *Paneer* as one of the most important foods.** But the tragedy lies in the fact that it is not consumed all over the country with the same gusto. It has come to stay as a North Indian food product. Inhabitants of the states of Jammu & Kashmir, Punjab, Haryana, Himachal Pradesh, Uttar Pradesh, Delhi, Rajasthan and Bihar, all enjoy hearty meals made of *Paneer*. In these parts of the country, it is commonly eaten in all the households in various forms by the vegetarians and non-vegetarians alike. They all prepare a variety of sweets and savouries too made of *Paneer*. There are no social gatherings or functions where some of the *Paneer* items are not served either as a snack, a sweet or a main dish. *Paneer* is stuffed in *Parathas, Kachoris* and *Samosas*. It is rolled into a variety of *Koftas*, turned into delicious

Tandoori Kababs and mixed with various vegetables. Spinach, Fenugreek, Green Peas, Capsicums and Mushrooms are a few to name. All the *Paneer*-based, commercially prepared Bengali sweets are also relished with the same spirit. So much so that now they have started stuffing even South Indian dishes like *Dosa* with *Paneer*. Uttapams with *Paneer* toppings are also finding place in the menus of hotels in South India. Broadly speaking, in the other states like Maharashtra, Gujarat, Andhra Pradesh, Karnataka, Kerala, Goa, Bengal, Orissa and Assam, *Paneer* is consumed but only in the form of famous Bengali sweets. People over there rarely mix *Paneer* with their *dals* and vegetable preparations. Ten years back, it was difficult to get *Paneer* from the market commercially in these states. But now, over a period, slowly but steadily a change is taking place. As most of the 'B' class cities are becoming cosmopolitan, availability of *Paneer* has increased, hotel culture is surmounting and people of all faiths have started enjoying *Paneer* delicacies while eating out. As a result, the popular dishes like *Palak Paneer*, *Paneer Tikkas* and *Paneer Parathas* are becoming household words. In Jammu area, *Paneer* is eaten in other interesting forms. The dried *Paneer* disks known as *Kaladis* are shallow fried, spiced with salt and red chilli powder and then consumed as a snack or along with the food. Though *Kaladi* is very tasty yet it is not commonly available.

Bengalis have got a sweet tooth. Amongst the other sweets, the *Chhena*-based sweets attract them more. Umpteen numbers of sweets are available in the Indian markets. As a result, packed *Rasogullas*, very popular Bengali sweets, are marketed all over the world and relished with the same gusto.

While writing this book, a lot of research work has been done and an effort has been made to cook the traditional *Paneer* in an untraditional but acceptably healthy ways. With the global changes all over the world and mixing of cultures, in modern times, it has become essential to revive the old style of Indian cooking, for instance, mixing *Paneer* with various fruits, vegetables and nuts; modifying traditional, regional gravies from all over India to cook *Paneer* with fruits and nuts making refreshing and healthy drinks with good old whey and using it as an excellent mineral water in the kitchen for various purposes, so that people of all ages, faiths and nationalities can enjoy the fruits of this versatile food item. These days Indian food is very popular abroad and all the nationalities are relishing its penchant flavour.

In this book, no doubt, a few popular dishes have been included whereas many of them (mostly the commercial ones) have been ignored, so that a number of healthier innovative dishes, which are tried and tested successfully for the benefit of users, can be enjoyed thoroughly. Therefore, not only cooking the dishes but their serving style and the accompaniments are also mentioned. Variations are given wherever necessary. Cooking tips along with some information about the dishes are also provided for the knowledge of the users. However, a fact remains that many hints have been taken from the food history while developing the recipes. Moreover, a special care has been taken to use the ingredients easily available in the Indian market and commonly used by the housewives, so that more number of people can utilize the recipes for the utility and variety in their cooking. Most of the gravies can be stored for many days under refrigeration in the deep freezer compartment. Working ladies can take the advantage and plan the meals properly.

Enjoy cooking these easy-to-follow *Paneer* recipes. Let your dear ones relish the variety because 'variety is the spice of life'.

Acknowledgement

Special thanks to my dear husband, Wg. Cdr. Mandhir Singh for his help at each stage in the making of this book. I would also like to thank my family, friends and well-wishers for their unrelenting support. Finally, I would like to dedicate this book to my inspiration, my brother, Late Mr. P S Kalsi.

Contents

DESSERTS

Introduction

Cattle were an integral part of the Vedic culture and literature before 800 BC and there is full reference of the milk of the cow, though that of buffalo and goat also finds mention in the Vedas. The cow is referred 700 times in the **'Rigveda'** alone as a symbol of bounty in numerous contexts. Milk, which was used during the Vedic period, was fresh, boiled, mixed with **Soma juice** or used as cream. It was used in various forms, e.g. as milk, curd, butter, whey, ghee and *Paneer*. During those times, *Paneer* was called *Dadhanwat*, with two forms with and without holes. Later on, it came to be known as *Chhena*-acid precipitated milk solids.

The Manasollasa written by king Someshwara of Central India in AD 1130 that deals with all the duties and recreation of a ruler among which are included matters relating to food and its preparation in the royal kitchen, recommends the addition of some sour substance to boiled milk, to get the precipitate and the whey separately. **Sour curds, limejuice and the whey kept from the previous run were generally used to get *Chhena*.** Earlier, solids were mixed with rice flour, fashioned into various shapes, fried in ghee and coated with sugar to get the delicacies like *Kshira Praka* or it was shaped into the likeness of the eggs of a peacock to prepare the delicacy, *Morendaka*. These two sweets are considered starting points for the whole range of modern Bengali sweets like *Kala Jamun, Sandesh, Sitabhog* and *Chhenar Jalebi*, etc. *Rasogulla* and *Rasmalai* appeared much later on the scene.

In the 21st century also, sour curds, lime juice and whey from the previous run are commonly used to get *Paneer* from milk, but the practice of employing citric acid crystals, known as *Tatri* and white vinegar is also popular to get *Paneer* from milk. For different uses in cookery, *Paneer* (*Chhena*/cottage cheese) is obtained from the cow's or buffalo's milk. For example: Cow's milk is preferred to make the popular Bengali delicacy like *Rasogulla* and to get solids for cooking savouries, buffalo's full cream milk is preferred. *Paneer* from cow's milk is supposed to have less fat contents. Commercially available *Paneer* is generally prepared from the full cream milk or buffalo's milk.

Paneer, a product of ancient heritage, is an excellent source of good quality high protein. Protein is one of the most important nutrients needed by the human body. It is the very basis of life and the only food substance that can repair and rebuild cells, thus restoring health and prolonged life. This food product contains all the essential amino acids, which feed our brain and the nervous system. It is a good protein for the stomach and helps in building the body. If the body is protein starved due to various reasons and the brain is tired, feed yourself with *Paneer* because Vitamin B-12 deficiency can lead to depression. *Paneer*, rich in vitamins A, B and E, contains calcium and is antipellagric. Vitamin B-12 which is found in plenty in animal foods, including fish, meat and eggs, is also available in abundance in milk and milk products. These days the depression due to Vitamin B-12, count is evident in young vegetarians and then vitamin injections are prescribed. Many young children suffer from this problem because either they do not take the balanced diet or do not eat regularly.

Since *Paneer* is an excellent vegetarian substitute, its consumption in our diet is essential to maintain a good health. You might be surprised to know that the people suffering from acidity are recommended to consume *Rasogullas*. Consumption of *Paneer* in any form is good for the ones who feel depressed and have lack of energy. Growing up children need vitamins more than the adults for bodybuilding, whereas grown ups need them for the maintenance of the body and its wear and tear. *Paneer* protein added to the vegetables and salads not only furnishes the dietry needs but also acts as a flavouring agent to enhance the less palatable taste of some vegetables. *Paneer* is the only protein which is easy on stomach and with which sour and sweet fruits and vegetables can be mixed easily and consumed without any loss of the natural contents. Uncooked *Paneer* marinated with lemon juice and consumed along with other food ingredients helps in digestion.

A few words about the excellent mineral water, the whey. It is rich in water soluble vitamins, minerals, trace elements and electrolytes. Any preparation made out of it is very nutritious and of low calorie. Food history shows that during the Vedic era, the whey was much in use. A popular refreshing drink was prepared by mixing it with some fruit juice and then flavoured with condiments. Nowadays, though people do not consume it as a refreshing drink, yet in India the people who know its value, do not waste it but use it to make *Chapati* dough or use it as a stock for the soups or gravies. In school days, we were taught that whey is an excellent food for children and adults suffering from stomach upset having water-like motions. Because of the above-mentioned qualities of whey, it stops dehydration and provides strength to the body.

Therefore, knowing the facts about such an excellent vegetarian substitute available within our reach, conscious effort should be made to learn the right combinations of food, not only to have variety in our diet but also to maintain a good standard of health of the dear ones. If proteins are eaten sensibly with more raw/cooked vegetables and fruits as salads than with more starches, no preparation can ever harm the system. People of all ages can enjoy it. To conclude, I must say that *Paneer* consumed as an important ingredient of diet with a variety of greens does wonders to the human system. We should always treat others and ourselves around us to the best because health is always within our reach if we are mentally prepared to learn from the experience.

A few words about Soyabean Cheese: Many people think that soyabean curd/bean curd cheese is like *Paneer* as far as the food value is concerned. No doubt, the bean curd, soyabean cheese or *Tofu* as the Chinese and Japanese call it respectively, is also a high protein food product which is made of soya milk. Bean curd is made of pureed and pressed soyabeans, its texture is like soft cheese. It remains fresh for several days if stored in water in a refrigerator. Like *Paneer*, it is sold in the form of cakes. To prepare soyabean cheese, they allow soya milk to curdle and set in a warm place. When it is soured and thickened, they bring it to a boil in a saucepan and then strain through a cloth. The soyabean is considered to be one of the richest of all foods in protein and in minerals. It also makes a very delightful addition to good meals. Like *Paneer*, it has an ancient heritage. This has been used for thousands of years by the people of the East, but American and European countries have started using it recently. Now they are considering it as a meat substitute. In India, soyabeans are best used as a spun protein like soyabean chunks and *Soya Kheema* which in turn are mixed with vegetables, added to the curries and turned into *Pulaos*. With the globalization, the food stores in bigger cities supply soya cheese or *Tofu* in the form of cakes and the star hotels are, of course, using it to create a variety of recipes. Those who are forbidden to consume the excellent milk food product, *Paneer*, due to some or the other medical reasons can consult their medical advisors and have soyabean cheese instead. In most of the recipes, wherever *Paneer* is used in chunks, soya cheese cubes can replace it. Like *Paneer*, *Tofu* can also be eaten raw/cooked mixed with salads or other suitable ingredients.

How to make *Paneer*

Ingredients

Full-cream Milk	1000 ml
Lime Juice	10 ml or
Lemon	1

Cooking

1. Boil milk with 1 cup water and add lime juice. The moment milk starts curdling, stir it once gently and switch off the fire.
2. Let it stand for 30 minutes to 1 hour. Strain it through a very fine sieve or a muslin cloth. Wait for 15 to 20 minutes and then use it or store it under refrigeration.

   Follow the same process with cow's milk or toned milk while making *Paneer*.

Yield

1. 1000 ml buffalo's full-cream milk will yield 2 and ¼ cup *Paneer* crumble.
2. 1000 ml cow's milk will give you 2 cups *Paneer* crumble.
3. 1000 ml toned or skimmed milk will give you 1 cup *Paneer* crumble.

Note

If you want to turn the *Paneer* crumble into a slab or a chunk, after straining the curdled milk through a muslin cloth to get the solids and whey separate, tie it up and place it under some weight for 1 hour. Then remove it from the cloth and store it under refrigeration. Cut into squares while using it. Please note, wherever *Paneer* crumble or grated *Paneer* is mentioned in the recipes, home-made *Paneer* can be ideally used.

If you are buying *Paneer* commercially, you can immerse the slab in water and store under refrigeration. This act will keep your *Paneer* fresh. But for the best results in cooking, always take *Paneer* out of the refrigerator and out of water at least 2 hours before use, so that it does not contain excess moisture.

Tips

Do not throw the 'whey' as it is an excellent mineral water, which can be converted into delicious and nourishing drinks and soups.

Variation

If you are planning to make stuffing for some savoury, you can add salt, pepper, green chilli and coriander chopped very fine to the boiling milk while curdling it.

Cooking time: 15 minutes.

For the best results in cooking, you must measure the ingredients required for any recipe accurately, so you must have the following aids in your kitchen:

- A set of Measuring Spoons
- A set of Measuring Cups
- A Measuring Jug

STARTERS

1. Cheese Coins

Ingredients

	(Serves 4-6 Persons)
Bread Slices	12
Paneer/Cottage Cheese	1 and ½ cup
Boiled Potato	1 no. large
Flour	1 tbsp
White Pepper Powder	2 tsp
Mint Powder	½ tsp
Grated Cheese	¼ cup + 2 tbsp
Green/Red Pepper	1 piece of 2"
Black Peppercorns	24
Salt	To taste

Preparation

1. Heat the oven for moderate heat.

2. With the help of a cutter or small *Katori*, cut the roundels out of bread slices.
3. Place the remaining portion of slices in an electric grinder and make fresh breadcrumbs.
4. Cut the pepper into 12 thin strips of ¾-inch long pieces.
5. Mix together *Paneer*/cottage cheese, potato, breadcrumbs, flour, mint, salt and pepper powder. Knead the mixture to fine dough.
6. Divide the dough into 12 portions.
7. Spread 1 portion of dough on 1 roundel of bread. Place 2 peppercorns as eyes and one small strip like a mouth. Finish making all the roundels this way.

Baking

Bake the roundels in hot oven for 10 to 15 minutes and remove.

Serving

Serve them hot or at room temperature with sauce as an evening snack. You may serve the roundels as starters at any gathering. In that case, cut them into 4 portions to make the bite-sized pieces.

Tips

Cheese coins are excellent for children or for their gatherings because children love the shapes and the crispness in any food.

Cooking time: 15 minutes for preparation and 15 minutes for baking.

2. Cheese Dossiers

Ingredients

(Serves 4-6 persons)

For Dossiers

Paneer/Cottage Cheese	1 cup
Flour	½ cup
Grated Cheese	¼ cup
Boiled Potato	2 (medium-sized)
Baking Powder	¼ tsp levelled
Pepper Powder	½ tsp
Salt	1 tsp
Tart Shells/Moulds	10-12

For Stuffing

Mushroom	6
Capsicum	2
Spring Onion	4

Parsley (Chopped)	2 tbsp
Paneer	½ cup
Tomato Sauce	2 tbsp
Pepper Powder	½ tsp
Grated Cheese	2 tbsp
Salt	To taste
Butter	2 tbsp

Preparation

1. Put the oven on for medium heat.
2. Mix together *Paneer*/cottage cheese, flour, potatoes, grated cheese for the dossiers, baking powder, salt and pepper. Knead well to pliable dough.
3. Roll the dough to ½ centimetre thick *Chapati* and cut the disks out of it to fit the tart moulds or small *Katoris*. Line the moulds with 1 disk each and prick it with a fork. Take out as many disks as you can. Roll the remaining dough once again and repeat the procedure till the dough finishes. Bake them blind for 15 minutes or till the edges turn brownish. Take them out of the oven and keep aside.

   This quantity of dough will give you 10 to 12 dossiers (baskets).

Baking

1. Meantime chop all the vegetables very fine for stuffing.
2. Heat butter in a pan and sauté onion in it. Then add chopped capsicum and mushroom. Once the vegetables are almost dry, add crumbled *Paneer* for the stuffing and the seasonings such as tomato sauce, grated cheese and chopped parsley. Mix well and remove from fire.

Serving

Divide the stuffing according to the number of baskets you baked. Stuff each basket with the stuffing, put a dot of sauce on top and serve at room temperature.

You can enjoy the dossiers with some extra sauce or any other *chutney*.

Cooking time: 20 minutes for preparation and 15 minutes for baking.

3. Paneer and Fruit Salad

Ingredients

	(Serves 4-6 Persons)
Paneer	250 gm
Black Grapes	1 cup
Green Grapes	½ cup
Mangoes	1
Cherry Tomatoes	½ cup
Pineapple	4 slices
Soaked Nuts	½ cup (optional)
Sesame Seeds	2 tbsp
Lettuce	6 to 8 leaves
Honey	¼ cup
Lemon Juice	2 tbsp
Salt	1 tsp
Pepper Powder	1 tsp
Mustard Powder	¼ tsp

Preparation

1. Cut *Paneer* into ½-inch cubes and marinate it with lemon juice, salt and pepper powder for 30 minutes.

2. Peel and cut mangoes into ½-inch pieces.
3. Cut pineapple slices also into ½-inch pieces.
4. Dry fry sesame seeds.
5. Chop the soaked nuts.
6. Immerse lettuce in cold water.

Mixing

Mix all the chopped fruits and nuts. Pour honey over them and toss well. Sprinkle mustard powder over the fruits and chill under refrigeration for a minimum time of 30 minutes.

Serving

Remove lettuce from water, pat it dry lightly with a kitchen towel and arrange the leaves in a platter. Mix the prepared fruits and marinated *Paneer* and place them in the centre of a lined platter. Arrange the cherry tomatoes around the pile of salad. Finally sprinkle the roasted sesame seeds on it and serve. The aroma of roasted sesame seeds makes this refreshing salad very special and appetizing.

Tips

You can mix *Paneer* cubes with any other seasonal fruits when mangoes or grapes are out of season. You may use oranges, apples, pears, papaya and soaked raisins. In winter season, you may avoid chilling the fruits. Adding soaked nuts like almonds, cashewnuts or walnuts not only enrich the taste of the salad but also add more food value to it. Dry fruits once soaked for 4 to 6 hours are revived and are easier to digest.

Cooking time: 15 minutes for preparation and 30 minutes for chilling.

4. Paneer Vadi Steamed

Ingredients

(Serves 4-6 Persons)

For Vadis

Paneer Grated	1 and ½ cup
Carrots Grated Fine	1 cup
Capsicum (Chopped)	2
Coriander (Chopped)	¼ cup
Onion (Grated)	1
Chilli Paste	1 tsp
Baking Soda	½ tsp
Gram Flour	½ cup
Salt	To taste
Asafoetida	A pinch (optional)

Tempering

Mustard Seeds	1 tsp
Oil	2 tsp

Preparation

1. Mix together grated *Paneer*, carrots, capsicum, onion, gram flour, chilli paste, coriander, baking soda and salt. Mix without water with vegetable juices only; if at all required, use a few drops. Mix properly and keep the mixture aside for 15 minutes.
2. Meantime, place a vessel for steaming. Grease the plate in which you are placing the mixture to be steamed.

Cooking

1. Steam *Paneer*, vegetables and gram flour mixture for 15 to 20 minutes. You may test it with a needle. If a needle inserted to check comes out clean, your mixture is cooked.

2. Remove from the steamer and cool it. Cut it into squares or diamond-shaped *Vadis* and place them in a shallow serving dish.
3. Heat oil for tempering and crackle mustard seeds in it. Pour this hot tempering oil with mustard seeds over the *Vadis*.

Serving

Serve *Paneer*-steamed *Vadis* at room temperature with any *chutney* or sauce. They taste excellent when cold, too.

Variation

Alongwith *Paneer* and gram flour, you may mix other vegetables like grated cauliflower or finely chopped spinach in the same proportion as carrots, etc.

Tips

- All the chopped vegetables should be finely grated.
- *Paneer* and vegetables to be used should be at room temperature.

Cooking time: 20 minutes for preparation and 20 minutes for steaming.

5. Refreshing Beverages (Whey Drinks)

Ingredients

	(Serves 4-6 Persons)
Whey	1000 ml
Pineapple juice	500 ml or
Mango Juice	500 ml

Sugar Powder	1 tsp each (optional)
Green Cardamom	6
Ginger powder	Optional
Crushed Ice	Optional
Tall Glasses	4 to 6

Preparation

1. Chill fresh whey.
2. Chill juice too.
3. Mix whey, juice and sugar. Stir well.
4. Remove the seeds from the cardamoms and powder them.

Serving

In each glass add 1 tbsp crushed ice and pour the mixed drink and finally sprinkle it with a pinch of cardamom powder. Place a stirrer in the glass and serve it chilled.

Use cardamom powder with pineapple juice and ginger powder with mango juice.

Variation

1. Instead of pineapple/mango juice, take grape juice. Follow the same procedure and serve the juice chilled.
2. Follow the same process but use *litchi* juice. In each glass, add a pinch of salt and black pepper powder too.
3. Use strawberry crush. Place whey and strawberry crush in an electric blender and churn for a while, strain and chill before serving.
4. Use 1000 ml whey, 150 ml Rooh Afza and juice of 1 lime. Chill and serve.
5. Add 2 tsp honey to 300 ml fresh hot whey and consume it during winters.
6. Use jaggery syrup instead of sugar and honey in the drinks.
7. Take 1 cup hot whey with lemon juice, salt or no salt and a pinch of white pepper powder. You may use cardamom or ginger powder with any juice of your choice.

Tips

- Whey is a rich source of water-soluble vitamins, minerals, trace elements and electrolytes. It is nutritious and low calorie mineral water.
- Whey drink was popular in India during the 12th century AD. It was prepared by adding citric fruit juices to boiled milk to separate the solids. After straining, it was mixed with some fruit juice and then flavoured with cardamom powder.

The pets are also fed on it. My dogs love eating *chapatis* with whey. For them, it is a substitute of milk.

Cooking time: 15 minutes for preparation plus the chilling time.

6. Cheesy Spinach Roundels

Ingredients

	(Serves 4-6 Persons)
Cottage Cheese	1 and ¼ cup
Spinach Puree	½ cup
Cheese (Grated)	½ cup
Flour	½ cup levelled
Cashew Nut	16
Baking Soda	¼ tsp levelled
Pepper Powder	2 tsp levelled
Salt	1 and ½ tsp levelled

Preparation

1. Sieve together flour, salt, pepper powder and baking soda.
2. Coarsely grind 10 cashew nuts and save 6 for topping.

3. Heat oven for moderate heat.
4. Mix together *Paneer*/cottage cheese, sieved flour, cashew nut powder and spinach puree. Knead to pliable dough. If you feel that dough is hard, sprinkle a few drops of milk and knead it again.
5. Divide the dough into 12 to 16 equal-sized portions. Roll each portion into a ball and then flatten it with your hands. This way roll and flatten all the portions. If, anyway, the dough sticks to your hands, smear your palms with a little butter or cooking oil and flatten the balls. The flattened roundels should be crack-free.
6. Place them on a baking tray at a distance of 4 inches.
7. Divide the saved cashew nuts into halves. Place one nut on each roundel.

Baking

Place the baking tray in the centre of the oven and bake the roundels for 20 to 25 minutes. Take out the tray and wait for 10 minutes. Remove the roundels and serve.

Serving

Serve them at room temperature with tomato sauce as a snack and with any cream salad at mealtime as a substitute of cutlet. This dish is an excellent accompaniment to a continental meal. Roundels seem cheesier when cold.

Tips

- For perfect baking, it is important that all the ingredients used are at room temperature while mixing. For instance, *Paneer*, spinach puree and cheese etc. should not be very cold, just taken out from the fridge.

- If *Paneer* and spinach are stored under refrigeration, they should be taken out at least 2 hours before use.
- Spinach puree should not be watery.

Cooking time: 15 minutes for preparation and 30 minutes for baking.

7. Hawaiian Salad

Ingredients

	(Serves 4-6 Persons)
Paneer	250 gm
Orange	2
Cucumber	1 to 2
Apple	1 large

Pineapple Slices	6
Lettuce	1 head

Dressing

Table Vinegar	¼ cup
Cooking Oil	1 tsp
Sugar	1 tsp
Salt	1 tsp
Mustard Powder	¼ tsp
Pepper Powder	1 tsp levelled

Preparation

1. Immerse lettuce in cold water.
2. Grate *Paneer*.
3. Peel orange and take out the pith out of the segments. Chop them into halves.
4. Peel and cut cucumber into ½-inch cubes.
5. Peel and core apple and then cut into cubes.
6. Cut the pineapple slices into halves. Chop half of the slices and save the other half for garnishing.

Mixing

1. Take out the lettuce out of water and pat the leaves dry. Arrange them in a salad platter. Firs pile up chopped cucumber and apple cubes, then pineapple and orange segments and, finally, pl the grated *Paneer* on top of everything. C
2. Mix all the ingredients for the dressing in a chill and shake well before use.

Serving

Take out the platter just before use and pour th dressing contents evenly over the arranged salad. Garnish with saved pineapple slices and serv immediately.

Cheese Coins

Cheese Dossiers

Paneer & fruit Salad

Cheesy spinach Roundels

Refreshing Beverages

Whey Tomato Celery Soup

Hawaian Salad

Paneer Phal Unli Kababs

Paneer Fruit Cocktails

Semolina Hearts

Whey Salad Mould

Paneer Kachori

Tips

- Lettuce or Cabbage leaves used for lining the salad platter are immersed in cold water for sometime to retain the crispness of the leaves.
- Always arrange salads with careful carelessness!

Cooking time: 20 minutes.

8. Paneer Phal Ungli Kababs

Ingredients

	(Serves 4-6 Persons)
Raw Banana	2
Paneer	1 and ½ cup

Roasted Gram Powder	¼ cup
Coriander (Chopped)	¼ cup
Green Chilli	4
Clove Powder	½ tsp levelled
Pepper Powder	1 tsp
Mint Powder	1 tsp
Mixed Nut Powder	4 tbsp
Salt	To taste
Oil	For frying

Preparation

1. Boil bananas in salted water, peel and mash.
2. Chop green chillies very fine.
3. Mix together *Paneer*, mashed bananas, chopped chillies, coriander, salt, roasted gram, clove, mint, pepper and mixed nut powders. Mash all the ingredients very well. Sprinkle a few drops of water if the dough is very dry and not binding well.
4. Divide the dough into 20 to 24 equal-sized portions. Roll each portion into ¾-inch thick finger. Finish rolling all the portions.

Cooking

1. Heat oil in a *Kadai* for frying to a smoking and then lower the heat.
2. Put 2 to 3 fingers at a time for frying and increase the heat. Fry the *Paneer* and banana fingers on medium fire.
3. Remove them on the kitchen paper for extra oil absorbance. Finish frying all the fingers.

Serving

Line a serving plate with lettuce or cabbage and arrange the fingers on it around a small bowl consisting of green chutney or tomato sauce.

Serve them hot.

Tips

- This preparation is an excellent snack for the rainy days and can be served as a starter for any party. For the party, you may roll bite-sized fingers.
- You may cook raw bananas in your microwave for 8 to 10 minutes.

Cooking time: 20 to 30 minutes for preparation and 20 minutes for frying.

9. Paneer and Fruit Cocktail

Ingredients

	(Serves 4-6 Persons)
Paneer	250 gm
Black Grapes	½ cup
Mango Pieces	½ cup
Cherry Tomatoes	½ cup or
Strawberries (Halved)	½ cup
Pineapple Titbits	½ cup or
Pickled Onion	½ cup or
Pickled Cucumber Chopped	½ cup
Lemon Juice	1 tbsp
White Pepper	1 tsp
Salt	½ tsp
Pack of Toothpicks	

Preparation

1. Cut *Paneer* into ½-inch cubes and marinate with lemon juice, salt and pepper powder for 30 minutes minimum before use.

2. Take one toothpick and pierce one grape or any one piece of strawberry/mango/pineapple, then a piece of marinated *Paneer* and finally another piece of fruit/cherry/tomato/pickled onion or a piece of cucumber.
3. This way create as many combinations as you can till the *Paneer* pieces last.

Serving

Arrange them in a plate or any other dish and serve as a starter in any gathering.

Tips

Along with *Paneer*, you can pick up any fruit or vegetable of your choice but for the good taste, one piece of fruit is essential in each stick.

Variation

- You can use fresh carrots, radish or mushrooms with *Paneer* for cocktails. If contrast-coloured eatables are used, aesthetically, first they appeal the eye and then satisfy the appetite!
- Along with marinated *Paneer* cubes, use pickled onions, capsicum and tomato pieces. Arrange them on toothpicks. Heat under grill just to warm them and serve immediately. The dish will be called *Paneer* Satte.

Cooking time: 20 minutes.

10. Whey Tomato Celery Soup

Ingredients

	(Serves 4-6 Persons)
Fresh Whey	600 ml
Tomato	3
Celery	2 sticks
Ginger	1-inch piece
Garlic	6 flakes
Green Chillies	2
Corn Flour	2 tbsp
Water	1 cup
Salt and Pepper	To taste

For Tempering

Cumin seeds	1 tsp
Butter/Oil	2 tsp

Preparation

1. Chop tomatoes, ginger, garlic and green chillies. Add 1 cup of water and grind through an electric grinder. Strain through a sieve and keep aside.
2. Chop celery very fine and add to the tomato mixture.

Cooking

1. Mix together tomato mixture and whey. Cook for 10 minutes.
2. Mix corn flour with ½-cup whey and add to the boiling soup. Cook for two minutes and remove from the fire. Check the seasonings and temper the soup.

Tempering

Heat oil in a ladle and crackle cumin in it. Pour it over the soup and serve it hot.

Serving

Serve the soup hot as a starter or along with the meal. This soup is very light, nourishing and pungent.

Variation

1. Instead of celery and chilli, you can add grated carrot and onion or ½ of a capsicum along with the tomatoes while grinding. Then follow the same process.
2. Use mixed vegetable stock with whey and temper it with finely chopped and fried garlic.

Cooking time: 10 minutes for preparation and 20 minutes for cooking.

11. Semolina Hearts

Ingredients

	(Serves 6-8 Persons)
Paneer Crumble	1 and ½ cup
Semolina	¾ cup
Milk/Coconut Milk	2 cups
Salt	2 tsp
Black Pepper Powder	1 tsp
Ginger Powder	1 tsp
Green Chillies (Chopped)	1 tbsp
Green Coriander (Chopped)	¼ cup
Peanut Powder	¼ cup
Boiled Potato	1
Flour	¼ cup (optional)
Oil	For frying

Preparation and cooking

1. Dry fry semolina on fire in an electric oven or even in a microwave to pinkish colour.
2. Add salt and pepper. Add milk or coconut milk and mix well. Remove from fire.
3. Handle it when it is cool enough.
4. Grate raw mango and boiled potato.
5. Add crumbled *Paneer*, boiled potato, chopped coriander, green chillies, ginger powder and grated raw mango. Mix well and knead it properly.
6. Add coarsely ground peanut powder and mix again. Sprinkle a few drops of water.

7. Divide the mixture into 12 to 16 equal portions and shape them like hearts. You may use heart-shaped mould, if available. In that case, fill up the mould tightly, taper it and slide the heart-shaped cutlet. This way shape all the portions and keep aside.

8. Heat oil for frying the hearts and then lower the heat.
9. Fry one or two pieces only at a time on medium fire, turn the side once and remove them on kitchen paper for extra oil absorbance. You may use the small frying baskets and fry one heart at a time.

Serving

Arrange the hearts on the bed of lettuce or cabbage leaves according to your imagination and serve them with any green chutney or tomato sauce.

Semolina hearts can be served with any good salad at any meal.

Tips

1. This dish is ideal even for those grown-ups who like to avoid potato cutlets for various reasons. These are excellent for children's lunch box, as an evening snack or even as a starter for the parties. If using them as starters, shape into small-sized hearts.
2. Use home-made *Paneer* for the preparation of this dish.

Cooking time: 30 minutes for preparation and 15 minutes for frying.

12. Whey Salad Mould

Ingredients

	(Serves 6-8 Persons)
Whey	500 ml
Salt	2 tsp

Pepper	2 tsp levelled
Gelatin	1 tbsp
Apple	1 medium-sized
Cucumber	1
Carrot	1
Capsicum	1 small
Mushroom	6
Paneer (Grated)	½ cup
Grapes	¼ cup
Ginger Powder	½ tsp levelled
Capsico	6 drops (optional)
Lemon	1

Preparation and Cooking

1. Boil whey with salt, pepper and ginger powder.
2. Mix gelatin with water, dissolve it on the pan of hot water and pour it over the hot whey.

3. Cool and place the pan in the deep freezer till the contents are half set like jelly.
4. Oil, rinse and place a glass bowl or a jelly mould in the freezer for chilling.
5. Meanwhile, peel, core and grate apple. Mix it immediately with the lemon juice to avoid discolouration.
6. Peel and grate cucumber and carrot too.
7. Wash and chop mushroom and capsicum very fine.
8. Clean and wash grapes.
9. In a separate bowl, mix all the prepared ingredients and also add grated *Paneer*.
10. Remove the half set-flavoured whey and just beat it with an eggbeater or a fork.
11. Now mix it properly with all the other ingredients.
12. Mix it lightly and pour in the chilled bowl.

Set it again in the freezer for 30 minutes or so. Remove and keep under refrigeration till used.

Serving

Serve the salad cold with Indian or continental meal.

Tips

1. If you want to unmould the salad, you may set it in an aluminium jelly mould and then dish out in a shallow glass dish that is chilled for the salad.
2. Only home-made fresh *Paneer* and whey should be used for this kind of salad.

Cooking time: 10 minutes. 15 minutes for preparation and 30 minutes for chilling.

13. Paneer Kachori

Ingredients

	(Serves 4-6 Persons)
Paneer	2 cups
Potatoes (Boiled)	4
Corn meal	¼ cup
Ajwain	½ tsp
Asafoetida	¼ tsp
Roasted Gram	2 tbsp
Roasted Sesame Seeds	2 tbsp
Green Chillies	3
Green Chilli Paste	1 tbsp
Garam Masala	½ tsp
Ginger	1-inch piece
Coriander (Chopped)	¼ cup
Black Salt Powder	To taste
Oil	For frying

Preparation

1. Mash together boiled potatoes, corn meal, ½ tsp salt and chilli paste. Knead and make smooth dough.
2. If the dough is not pliable enough, sprinkle a little warm water and knead it once more.
3. Chop green chillies and ginger very fine.
4. Powder roasted gram and sesame seeds coarsely.

Cooking

1. Heat ½ tsp oil and crackle *ajwain* in it. Switch off the heat and add asafoetida.
2. Mix together *Paneer*, black salt, *garam masala*, chopped ginger, green chilli, roasted gram and coriander. Pour over it crackled *ajwain* and asafoetida. Mix well.
3. Divide the potato-corn meal dough into equal portions. Take one ball and flatten it on your hand or on a chopping board, place 2 tsp stuffing in it and seal it. Slightly press to flatten it. This way finish stuffing all the *kachoris.*
4. Heat oil for frying. Fry 1 or 2 *kachoris* only at a time on medium flame till golden brown in colour. Lift from the oil with a slotted spoon and place them on kitchen paper for extra oil absorbance.

Serving

Serve *Kachoris* hot with any green chutney or tamarind sauce. You can eat plain curds also with this preparation.

Variation

Instead of potato and corn meal for the outer covering, make dough with 200 gm flour, 50 gm semolina, 3 tbsp oil and ½ tsp salt. Rest follow the same process.

Tips

Make green chutney with 1 cup fresh coriander, 1 onion, 4 green chillies and 1 small raw mango or juice of 1 big lime. Chop everything and grind together to a smooth paste. Add salt to taste. Store under refrigeration.

Cooking time: 30 minutes for preparation and 30 to 40 minutes for frying.

14. Salad 'C' Plus

Ingredients

	(Serves 4-6 Persons)
Cottage Cheese	150 gm
Carrot	1
Cucumber	1
Capsicum (Red)	1 small
Cabbage Leaves	4
Chillies (Green)	2
Capsico	4 drops
Cherry Tomatoes	16 (optional)
Pineapple slices	4 (optional)
Peanuts (Soaked)	½ cup
Moong (Sprouts)	½ cup
Lemon	2
Pepper Powder	1 tsp
Spring Onions	4
Mustard Seeds	1 tsp
Asafoetida	A pinch
Salt	1 tsp
Oil	2 tsp

Preparation

1. Grate cottage cheese/*Paneer* and carrot. Mix with ½ tsp salt, ½ tsp pepper powder and juice of 1 lemon. Keep aside.
2. Remove the spine of cabbage leaves and roll them together. Cut them very fine and immerse in cold water for 20 minutes.
3. Chop red capsicum, cucumber, chillies and pineapple slices very fine.
4. Cut cherry tomatoes in halves.
5. Cut spring onions in rings and soak in water for sometime.
6. Squeeze another lemon and collect the juice.

Mixing

Take out cabbage and spring onions out of water and place them in a strainer. Meanwhile, in a big salad bowl, mix all the chopped ingredients for the 'C' plus salad. Add soaked peanuts and sprouts. Dry the cabbage leaves and onions and place them also in the bowl. Sprinkle lemon juice, salt, pepper powder and capsico drops. Toss the salad ingredients. Now mix grated *Paneer* and carrot with the other ingredients lightly.

Tempering

Finally, heat 2 tsp oil and crackle mustard in it. Switch off the fire and add a pinch of asafoetida. Pour this tempering over the salad and toss it once again.

Serving

Serve it in the salad bowl or line a platter with lettuce and pile up the salad in the centre. Garnish the way you prefer.

Cooking time: 30 minutes.

15. Paneer Fingers

Ingredients

	(Serves 4-6 Persons)
Paneer	300 gm
Lemon Juice	10 ml
Salt	1 tsp
Chilli Powder	1 tsp

For Batter

Gram Flour	1 cup
Corn Flour	1 tbsp
Ajwain	½ tsp
Baking Soda	¼ tsp
Garam Masala	½ tsp

Garlic Paste	1 tsp
Green Chilli Paste	1 tsp
Coriander (Chopped)	¼ cup
Black Salt	¼ tsp
Salt	2 tsp
Oil	For frying
Chaat Masala	1 to 2 tsp for topping

Preparation

1. Cut *Paneer* into 6 cms × 2 cms long and thick fingers respectively. Sprinkle 1 tsp salt, lime juice and red chilli powder. Toss lightly and keep aside.
2. Mix together gram flour, 1 tsp salt, corn flour, baking soda, black salt, *Ajwain*, chilli paste and coriander.
3. Mix it with water to a thick batter. Keep aside and let it stand for 30 minutes.

Cooking

1. Heat oil for frying *Paneer* fingers. Bring oil to a smoking point and then lower the heat.
2. Beat the gram flour batter with your hand for a few seconds. Add a little water if the batter is too thick. It should be of thick pouring consistency.
3. Dip each marinated *Paneer* finger into the gram flour batter properly and put in hot oil. Increase the heat to a medium level in the gas stove. Put 3 to 4 fingers only at a time for frying.
4. Turn the side once. Fry the *Paneer* fingers to golden brown colour, remove and place them on the kitchen paper for extra oil absorbance. This way finish frying all the fingers.

Serving

Sprinkle *Chaat Masala* over the *Paneer* fingers and serve them hot with green *chutney* or tomato sauce.

Tips

You may avoid *Chaat Masala* if you don't take extra salt.

Variation

Marinate *Paneer* the way it is mentioned above. Instead of making gram flour batter, take half the quantity of gram flour and rest of the ingredients for the batter. Mix them dry and sprinkle over the *Paneer* pieces. Toss them lightly till the gram flour absorbs all the moisture. Fry the way it is mentioned.

Cooking time: 30 minutes for preparation and 30 minutes for frying.

16. Cheese Frankies

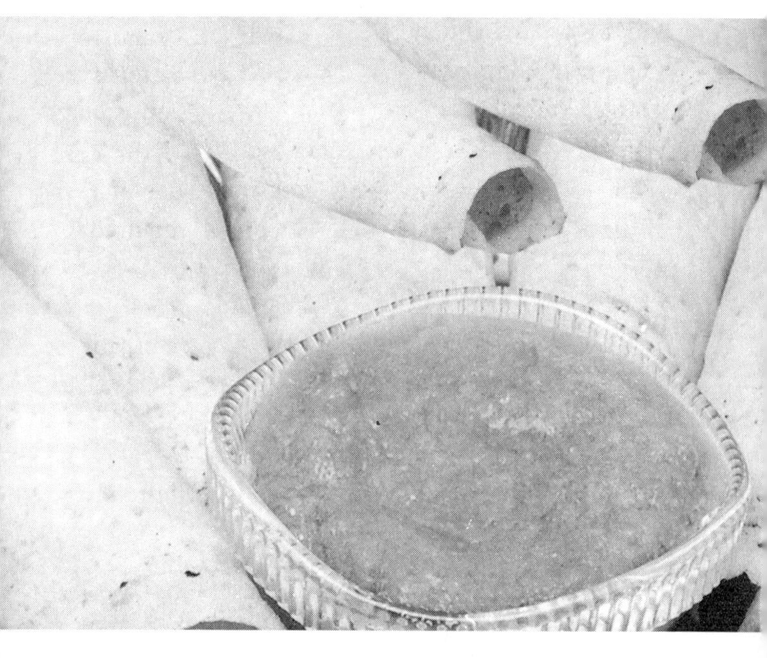

Ingredients

(Serves 4-6 Persons)

For Frankie

Gram Flour	1 and ½ cup
Whey	2 cups
Ginger Powder	¼ tsp (Levelled)
Asafoetida	¼ tsp (Levelled)
Baking Soda	¼ tsp
Salt	1 tsp
Chilli Powder	½ tsp
Mint Powder	½ tsp
Oil	2 tbsp

For Stuffing

Paneer/cottage Cheese	1 cup

Grated Cauliflower	1 cup
Spring Onion With Greens	6
Green Chillies	4
Chopped Coriander	¼ cup
Chopped Ginger	2 tsp
Pepper powder	½ tsp
Ajwain	½ tsp
Tomato Sauce	2 tbsp
Milk	¼ cup, if required
Oil	2 tbsp

Preparation

1. Mix together all the ingredients for the Frankie, except oil. Beat it well with any beater and keep aside for 30 minutes minimum.
2. Meanwhile, prepare the stuffing. Chop onions and green chillies.

Cooking

1. Heat 2 tbsp oil in a pan and crackle *Ajwain* in it.
2. Add chopped chillies and onions; sauté till pinkish in colour.
3. Now put grated cauliflower in it and stir on high flame. Add salt and pepper and cook for a while. Add crumbled *Paneer* and mash well. Sprinkle milk over the stuffing if it appears dry.
4. Put tomato sauce in the mixture and mix well.
5. Finally sprinkle chopped coriander, remove from fire and keep it covered.
6. Heat a griddle or a non-stick pan, smear it with a drop of oil and lower the heat under it.
7. Beat the gram flour batter once again. Put 1 ladle full of batter on griddle and tilt it, so that the batter spreads evenly. Cook on full flame, sprinkle a little oil and turn the side and cook for a while.

Remove from the pan and keep it warm in a container. This way cook all the pancakes from both sides (for Frankie) and keep them warm.

8. Now stuff them one by one and roll. For stuffing, place one pancake on the chopping board, and spread one tbsp stuffing evenly on it and roll it. Finish stuffing all the pancakes.

Serving

Serve the Cheese Frankie warm at room temperature with tomato sauce or green *chutney*.

This dish is just ideal for the evening snack or it can be served for breakfast along with porridge and fruit or it can be carried in the lunch box.

Tips

For the preparation of this dish, home-made cottage cheese is used. *Paneer* is used for the stuffing and its whey is consumed to make the batter for the pancakes.

Variation

- You may add any other vegetables of your choice to the *Paneer* for the stuffing, for example, chopped mushroom, capsicum or grated carrot. Then adjust the seasonings accordingly.
- If you like to eat plain gram flour pancakes, add chopped coriander and one (1) grated onion to the batter.
- Use buttermilk instead of whey for making batter. Rest follow the same recipe.

Cooking time: 15 minutes for preparation and 35 minutes for cooking.

17. Paneer Rolls

Ingredients

	(Serves 4-6 Persons)
Boiled Potatoes	4
Crumbled *Paneer*	1 cup
Bread Slices	4
Coriander (Chopped)	¼ cup
Green Chillies	4
Mango Powder	1 tsp (Levelled)
Ginger Powder	½ tsp (Levelled)
Chilli Powder	1 tsp (Levelled)
Pepper Powder	½ tsp
Salt	To taste
Green Peas	1 cup
Grated	Cheese ¼ cup
Salt	¼ tsp
Oil	For frying

Preparation

1. Break the bread slices into pieces.
   Put them in an electric grinder and make fresh breadcrumbs.
2. Chop green chillies very fine.
3. Mash together boiled potatoes, crumbled *Paneer* and breadcrumbs.
4. Add salt, chilli, mango and ginger powder. Mix chopped green chillies and ¾ chopped coriander. Knead well and divide into 12 to 16 equal portions. Keep aside.

Cooking

1. Heat 1 tbsp oil in a pan and sauté green peas in it. Add salt, pepper and the remaining coriander in it. When peas are dry, remove and mix the grated cheese.
2. Heat oil for deep-frying. Bring it to the smoking point and then lower the heat.
3. Take one portion of the *Paneer*-potato mixture, flatten it and place 1 tsp green peas mixture in the centre of it and roll it lengthwise. This way stuff and roll all the portions.
4. Increase the heat under oil and fry the rolls to golden brown colour. Fry 1 roll only at a time and place on the kitchen paper. Finish frying all the rolls.

Serving

Cut them into halves diagonally. Arrange the rolls in a plate lined with lettuce and serve hot with any *chutney* or sauce.

Variation

Instead of green peas and cheese stuffing, place a piece of cheese in the centre of the roll. Make stuffing with other vegetables or mutton or chicken mince.

Tips

These rolls can easily be served with any continental menu in place of cutlets. You can serve these rolls with *chutney,* sauce or with salads containing fresh vegetables such as carrots (gajar), raddish *(mooli),* onions, tomatoes, etc.

Cooking time: 20 minutes for preparation and 20 minutes for frying.

MAIN COURSE

1. Corn-*Paneer* Kofta in Rajasthani Gravy

Ingredients

(Serves 4-6 Persons)

For Rajasthani Gravy

Tomato Puree	2 cups
Chilli-Garlic Sauce	½ cup
Butter	4 tbsp
Ajwain	1 tsp
Chopped Basil *(Tej Patta)*	1 tsp
Cream	¼ cup (optional)
Garam Masala	1 tsp
Sugar	1 tsp
Chopped Coriander *(Dhania)*	¼ cup

For Corn-*Paneer* Kofta

Tender Corn or Cobs	2
Paneer (Crumble)	1 cup
Gram Flour	¼ cup
Green Chillies	2
Garam Masala	1 tsp
Chilli Powder	1 tsp
Salt	1 tsp
Oil	For frying

Preparation and Cooking

1. Grate corn and mix with *Paneer* crumble and all the other ingredients for *Koftas* except oil for frying. Do not add water. Mix well and make lemon-sized balls. This recipe will give you 12 to 14 *Koftas*. Hard corn can be partly boiled before grating.
2. Heat oil for frying to the smoking point, lower the heat and then fry 2 to 3 corn-*Paneer Koftas* at a time on medium flame. Remove and place them on kitchen paper.

   Note: You may serve them as a starter or a snack.
3. Heat butter for gravy and crackle *Ajwain*.
4. Add tomato puree and cook for 5 minutes.
5. Put chilli-garlic sauce and half the chopped coriander in tomato puree and further cook it till the oil separates.
6. Add 2 cups of water. Boil and then reduce the heat, simmer the gravy for 10 minutes.
7. Add sugar and basil, cover the dish and switch off the fire. Check the salt.

Serving

Place the Corn-*Paneer Koftas* in a shallow serving dish, pour the garlic-flavoured chilli hot Rajasthani gravy around them and garnish with the remaining coriander and serve hot. The best accompaniment to this dish is *Do Palli Ki Roti* or boiled rice.

Variation

Cook vegetable sizzler or marinated chicken or mutton with this spicy gravy.

Tips

Always place soft *koftas* in the gravy just before serving, otherwise *koftas* will be too soft to be handled. Reheat gravy, if required, before serving. Reheat the *Koftas* before serving if prepared earlier but not with the gravy unless mentioned in a recipe.

Cooking time: 15 minutes for preparation and 30 minutes for cooking.

2. Paneer Methauries

Ingredients

(Serves 4-6 Persons)

For Methauries

Paneer	Grated 1 cup
Methi Leaves (Cooked)	1 cup
Corn Meal (*Makki Ka Atta*)	1 and ½ cup
Ajwain	½ tsp
Baking Soda	A pinch
Chilli-garlic Paste	2 tsp
Salt	To taste
Oil	For frying

For Rayta

Curd	3 cups
Oranges	4
Sugar Powder	2 to 3 tbsp
Pepper Powder	1 tsp
Cardamom Powder	½ tsp
Salt	To taste

Preparation

1. Beat curd along with sugar, pepper and cardamom powder and keep under refrigeration for cooling.
2. Peel orange, clean, remove the piths and cut the segments into small pieces.
3. Add salt to the curd and mix the orange segments too. Cool the *Rayta* till required.
4. Mix together corn meal, *Paneer*, *methi* leaves, *ajwain*, baking soda, chilli, garlic and salt.
5. Knead well and divide the dough into 16 portions.

Roll them on folded kitchen napkin into 4-inch disks. Use a little dry corn meal to sprinkle on the folded napkin while rolling the *Methauries*.

Cooking

1. Heat oil for frying to the smoking point and then lower the heat.
2. Fry the rolled *Paneer Methauries* one by one.
3. Put it in the oil and increase the heat. Turn it once so that it puffs well and gets evenly crisp. Fry it to golden brown colour.
4. Remove and place it on the kitchen paper so that the paper absorbs extra oil.
5. Finish frying all *Methauries* and serve.

Serving

Serve the *Methauries* hot and relish them with orange *Rayta*.

This dish is ideal for breakfast or as a holiday special brunch.

Variation

If you and your family members do not like fried *Methauries* for any reason, cook them on hot *Tava* from both the sides and serve with orange *Rayta*.

Tips

A 16th century work lists foods of the Gangetic Plains of Uttar Pradesh and Bihar; and *Methauri* is one of the popular fried preparations. Here, just from a single line description in the food history, we prepared this innovative dish of *Paneer*, *Methi* and corn meal and *Poories* are the best accompaniments.

Cooking time: 15 to 20 minutes for preparation and another 15 minutes for frying.

3. *Paneer* Tikki with Kesari Gravy

(A rich dish of cottage cheese and nuts from Punjab)

Ingredients

(Serves 4-6 Persons)

For *Paneer* Tikki

Paneer	250 gm
Cashew Nuts	¼ cup
Raisins	¼ cup
Coriander (Chopped)	½ cup
Ginger (Grated)	2 tbsp
Green Chilli	6
Garam Masala	1 tsp
Corn Flour	2 tbsp (Levelled)

Nutmeg Powder	A pinch
Cardamom Powder	½ tsp
Cream	¼ cup
Mint (Chopped)	2 tbsp
Salt	To taste
Oil	For frying *Tikkis*

For Kesari Gravy

Almonds	20 gm
Cashew Nuts	50 gm
Cream	½ cup
Curd	½ cup
Lime Juice	1 tbsp
White Peppercorns	1 tsp
Green Chillies	3
Black Cumin	½ tsp
Green Cardamom	4
Cloves	4
Saffron	A few strands
Yellow Chilli Powder	1 tsp
Butter	100 gm
Ginger paste	1 tbsp
Bay Leaf *(Tej Patta)*	1
Water	1 and ½ cup
Coriander *(Dhania)*	A few sprigs

Preparation for Tikki

1. Grate *Paneer*.
2. Chop cashew nuts, raisins and green chillies.
3. Mix together all the ingredients for *Tikki* to a soft dough. Divide into equal portions and flatten them like *Pattis.* Keep aside.

For Gravy

1. Soak cashew nuts in hot water for 15 minutes.
2. Blanch almonds.

Salad Cheese Plus

Paneer Fingers

Cheese Frankies

Paneer Methauries

Corn Paneer Kofta

Paneer Rolls

Paneer Kofta Kadi

Paneer Tikki with Kesri Gravy

Dhingri Dolma

Chettinad Paneer

Tava Paneer

Paneer in Andhra Gravy

3. Grind almonds and cashew nuts to a fine paste.
4. Pound cardamoms, cloves and pepper to a fine powder.
5. Chop chillies and coriander.
6. Beat curd and soak saffron in 2 tbsp of milk or water.

Cooking

1. Heat oil for frying *Paneer* Tikkies, lower the heat and then fry.

   Fry 1 to 2 pieces only at a time on medium fire.

   Remove and place them on kitchen paper for extra oil absorbance.

   Note: *Paneer Tikki* can be served as an appetizer/starter with *chutney* or sauce.

   You may shallow fry Tikkis.
2. Heat butter and crackle black cumin in it.
3. Add ginger paste and cook till pinkish in colour.
4. Add almond and cashew pastes and fry till oil separates.
5. Add chopped chillies and curd.
6. Now put water, salt, bay leaf, cardamom powder, *garam masala* and yellow chilli powder. Simmer the gravy for 10 minutes. It should have a soup-like consistency.
7. Now mix lemon juice, cream and saffron. Bring it to a boiling point and remove from fire.

Serving

Arrange the fried *Paneer Tikkies* in a shallow ovenproof dish and pour *Kesari Gravy* over and around them. Garnish with chopped coriander and 1 tbsp cream. Serve hot or at room temperature along with hot *Tandoori Roti* or fresh roasted *Phulkas*.

If you want to heat the dish, heat it before garnishing.

Variation

You may add *Paneer* pieces to the Kesari Gravy instead of *Paneer Pattis.* The dish will be called ***Paneer* Kesari.**

Tips

1. For this variation, cut *Paneer* into 1-inch square pieces and boil them in salted water for 5 minutes to which a pinch of turmeric is also added. Drain and add to the gravy. By boiling it in water beforehand, *Paneer* remains softer even in thicker gravy.

   Please note that this gravy is without onions, tomatoes and garlic. The gravy gets the body from almond and cashew pastes and flavour from the spices.
2. Without saffron and yellow chilli powder, the gravy is **"Basic White Gravy"** which is the base of many more gravies.

Cooking time: 30 minutes for preparation and 40 minutes for cooking.

4. Dhingri-Dolma in Almond Gravy

Ingredients

	(Serves 4-6 Persons)
Mushroom	100 gm
Paneer	200 gm
Almonds	20
Onion	3

Tomato	2
Ginger Paste	2 tbsp
Green Chilli	4
Green Cardamom	3
Cinnamon Powder	½ tsp
White Pepper Powder	1 tsp
Cloves	6
Thick Curd	½ cup
Oil/Butter	¼ cup
Asafoetida	¼ tsp
Aniseed	1 tsp
Kashmiri Chilli	1 tsp
Cream	¼ cup
Salt	To taste

(From Jammu and Kashmir)

Preparation

1. Blanch almonds and grind them with thick curd to a fine paste.

2. Cut and paste tomatoes and green chillies through an electric grinder and strain.
3. Peel and slice onions. Heat oil and fry them. Mix them with tomato puree and grind to a fine paste.
4. Cut mushroom into halves and *Paneer* into 1-inch square pieces. Mix and marinate them with 1 tsp salt and 1 tsp white pepper powder.
5. Roast aniseeds and powder.

Cooking

1. Heat oil used for frying onions and crackle cloves and green cardamoms in it. Add ginger paste and fry for a few seconds.
2. Now put onion and tomato paste in it and fry till the oil separates.
3. Put 2 cups water, almond paste, cinnamon, aniseed powder and asafoetida. Bring the gravy to a boiling point and then simmer it for 15 minutes. Now add the marinated *Paneer* and mushroom.
4. After 10 minutes, add cream to the gravy and simmer for another 5 minutes. Add ¼ cup boiled water if you find the gravy too thick. Stir.
5. Remove from fire and transfer it to a serving dish with a lid. Temper it just before serving.

Serving

Heat 1 tsp oil or ghee, switch off the fire and add *Kashmiri* chilli powder in it. Immediately pour the tempering over *Dhingri-Dolma.* Cover with the lid for a while. The best accompaniment to this dish is either *Jeera Rice* or *Kashmiri Roti.*

Variation

Instead of adding *Paneer* in pieces, just grate it into the gravy with mushroom in it.

Cooking time: 30 minutes for preparation and 30 minutes for cooking.

5. Paneer Kofta Kadi

Ingredients

(Serves 4-6 Persons)

For Koftas

Paneer Crumble	1 cup
Gram Flour	¼ cup
Baking Soda	A big pinch
Ajwain	¼ tsp
Ginger Powder	½ tsp
Garam Masala	1 tsp
Green Chillies	3
Chopped Coriander/Mint	2 tbsp
Salt	To taste

For Kadi

Buttermilk	1000 ml
Gram flour	¼ cup
Asafoetida	A big pinch
Turmeric Powder	1 tsp
Salt	2 tsp
Chopped Garlic	1 tbsp

Tempering

Fenugreek Seeds	½ tsp
Mustard Seeds	¼ tsp
Cumin	¼ tsp
Cloves	4
Curry Leaves	2 sprigs
Oil	1 tbsp

Preparation and Cooking

1. Mix together buttermilk, gram flour, asafoetida, turmeric and salt in a blender. Strain and place on fire, cook on high flame till it comes to the boiling point. Lower the heat and let it simmer.
2. Mix together *Paneer*, gram flour, *ajwain*, baking soda, salt, *garam masala*, green chillies and chopped coriander or mint leaves. Knead well and divide into 16 equal parts. Make smooth balls.
3. Bring *Kadi* to a boiling point and drop rolled *Koftas* in it. First 5 minutes let them boil on high flame, then lower the heat and let them simmer with *Kadi* for 15 minutes. Add ¼ cup water if Kadi starts thickening.
4. Heat oil for tempering the *Kofta Kadi*. Crackle cloves and take out. Cool and powder them.
5. In the same oil, first add mustard seeds and cumin for crackling, then fenugreek seeds and finally chopped garlic and curry leaves.

6. Remove the cooked preparation from fire and transfer it to the serving bowl.

Serving

Pour the tempering over *Koftas* and serve hot with plain boiled rice.

Variation

Put Koftas in a boiling thin gravy like *Punjabi Tari* and simmer for 15 minutes.

Tips

This dish is very light. It contains only 1 tbsp of oil and so everyone can enjoy it.

Cooking time: 10 minutes for preparation and 20 minutes for cooking.

6. *Paneer* Chettinad

Ingredients

	(Serves 4-6 Persons)
Paneer	500 gm
Tomato	4
Onion	3
Urad Dal	2 tbsp
Fenugreek Seeds	2 tsp
Cloves	4
Cinnamon Stick	1-inch piece
Cardamoms	6
Bay Leaf	1
Curry Leaves	1 sprig
Cooking Oil	¼ cup
Salt	To taste

For Fine Paste

Peppercorns	20
Cumin	1 tsp
Turmeric	1 tsp
Cashew Nuts	20
Poppy Seeds	2 tsp
Ginger Paste	2 tsp
Garlic Paste	2 tsp
Fenugreek Seeds	1 tsp
Red Chillies Whole	6

(From Chennai Area)

Preparation

1. Soak Urad Dal.
2. Cut *Paneer* into 1-inch square pieces, sprinkle with 1 tsp salt and toss gently.
3. Slice onions.

4. Blanch tomatoes and puree.
5. Grind all the ingredients mentioned for fine paste with ½ cup water.

Cooking

1. Heat oil and put urad dal in it. Stir and add whole spices like cardamoms, cloves, cinnamon stick, fenugreek seeds and curry leaves. Fry on slow fire and crackle the spices.
2. Add sliced onions and fry till golden brown.
3. Add tomato puree and bay leaf. Cook it till the oil separates.
4. Now mix ground masala with it and fry. Add the *Paneer* pieces and 2 and ½ cups of water. Bring it to the boiling point. Lower the heat and simmer till the dish is almost dry. Remove from fire and serve hot.

Serving

Paneer Chetttinad is a dry dish. So serve it with plain *Dosa* or *Paratha*.

Variation

Cook chicken with the same gravy.

Tips

Chettiyar is a place near Chennai and this exotic dish flavoured with black pepper is a specialty of the Chettiyar community.

Cooking time: 30 minutes for preparation and 20 minutes for cooking.

7. Tava Paneer

Ingredients

	(Serves 4-6 Persons)
Paneer	500 gm
Lime Juice	2 tbsp
Red Chilli Powder	1 tbsp
Turmeric Powder	1 tbsp
Salt	2 tsp

For Tava Gravy

Onion	4
Tomato	4
Capsicum	2
Green Chilli	4
Ginger	3-inch piece
Coriander (Chopped)	¼ cup
Cumin	1 tsp

Garam Masala	1 tbsp
Cooking Oil	¼ cup
Salt	To taste

Preparation

1. Cut *Paneer* into 1-inch squares. Marinate them with lemon juice, salt, red chilli and turmeric powder. Toss lightly and keep aside for 30 minutes, minimum.
2. Meantime, dice capsicums and tomatoes.
3. Slit green chillies.
4. Shred ginger or cut it into juliennes.
5. Slice onions thinly.

Cooking

1. Heat oil on a thick-bottomed *tava*. Fry sliced onions till it is crisp. Then remove and keep aside.
2. In the same oil, crackle cumin and add diced capsicums and tomatoes. Sauté well.
3. Add marinated *Paneer* pieces, fried onions, slit green chillies and ginger juliennes. Mix with a light hand, cover and cook for 5 minutes so that the *Paneer* absorbs the aroma of the *tava masala*.
3. Uncover and adjust seasonings, if required.
4. Sprinkle *Garam Masasla*. Mix lightly and avoid breaking *Paneer* pieces.

Serving

Dish out and serve it hot garnished with chopped coriander.

Enjoy the mild taste of the dish with *Paratha/ Tandoori Roti* or *Naan.*

Variation

1. Add halved mushroom in addition, and the dish will be known as ***Vegetable Jal Fraize***.

2. You may cook chicken in the same gravy but marinate it for 4 to 6 hours in advance.

Cooking time: 30 minutes for preparation and 15 minutes for cooking.

8. *Paneer* cooked in Andhra gravy

Ingredients

	(Serves 4-6 Persons)
Onion	3
Red Chilli (Whole)	3
Green Chilli	4
Peanuts	¼ cup
Coconut (Grated)	¼ cup

Curd	½ cup
Tamarind	A lemon-sized ball
Ginger Paste	1 tbsp
Garlic Paste	1 tsp
Coriander Seeds	1 tsp
Cloves	6
Green Cardamom	6
Cinnamon Stick	1-inch piece
Red Chilli Powder	1 tbsp
Turmeric	1 tsp
Mustard Seeds	½ tsp
Fenugreek Seeds	¼ tsp
Water	300 ml
Oil	3 tbsp
Curry Leaves	1 sprig
Paneer	300 gm
Sesame Seeds	1 tsp
Oil	1 tsp
Lemon	1
Salt	To taste

Preparation

1. Dry fry peanuts. Cool them and then remove the husk.
2. Chop onion and green chillies very fine. Deseed the red chilli (whole).
3. Soak tamarind in hot water for sometime, mash and take out the pulp.
4. Grind together coconut, peanuts, coriander and fenugreek seeds, cloves, green cardamoms, cinnamon and curd to a fine paste.
5. Cut *Paneer* into 1-inch squares and sprinkle 1 tsp salt and juice of a lemon over it. Toss it lightly and keep aside.

Cooking

1. Heat oil, crackle mustard in it and add curry leaves, chopped onions and green chillies. Fry till the onion is golden brown.
2. Add ginger and garlic paste and cook for a minute.
3. Add ground peanut, coconut and spice mixture; fry till the oil separates. If the *masala* sticks to the bottom, sprinkle a few drops of water every now and then.
4. Add 2 cups of water, *Paneer* pieces, chilli powder, turmeric and 1 tsp salt. Simmer the gravy for 20 minutes. Add tamarind or lemon.
5. Remove from fire and adjust the salt.

Serving

Heat 1 tsp ghee, crackle 1 tsp sesame seeds in it and temper the dish with it (optional). Serve the dish hot with *Lemon Rice.*

Cooking time: 25 minutes for preparation and 30 minutes for cooking.

9. *Paneer* and Mixed Vegetable Sizzler

Ingredients

	(Serves 4-6 Persons)
Paneer	300 gm
Mushroom	200 gm
Carrot	3
Green Pepper	3
Red Pepper	1

Yellow Pepper	1
Lemon	1
Cauliflower/Broccoli	1 head
Cabbage	1 head
Baby Potatoes	16
Garlic Flakes	10
Coriander (Chopped)	¼ cup
Tomato Puree	1 cup
Chilli Sauce	¼ cup
Ginger Powder	1 tsp
Black Peppercorns	10
Soya sauce	2 tsp
Oil	3 tbsp
Butter	2 tbsp
Sizzler Plate	2 to 4
Salt	To taste

Preparation

1. Squeeze lime and collect its juice. Cut *Paneer* into 1-inch cubes and marinate with lime juice and 1 tsp of salt.
2. Wash, dry and cut mushroom into halves.
3. Cut all the peppers too into 1-inch pieces.
4. Scrape and cut carrots into roundels.
5. Break cauliflower or broccoli into flowerets.
6. Chop garlic very fine. Crush peppercorns coarsely.
7. Take out the cabbage leaves, wash and dry.

Cooking

1. Boil baby potatoes and peel. Steam or boil carrots and cauliflower pieces with a pinch of salt. Do not overcook.
2. Heat oil, fry chopped garlic and coriander. Add peppercorns and stir. Put chopped peppers and mushroom in it and fry for a minute. Lift the vegetables out with a slotted spoon and keep aside.
3. In the same pan, add tomato puree, chilli sauce, ginger powder and 1 tsp salt. Stir for 2 minutes.
4. Add boiled vegetables and marinated *Paneer* pieces. Cook them till the vegetables are well coated with the *masala* and the water is almost dry.
5. Add Soya sauce, fried peppers and mushroom. Mix gently and remove from fire.

Serving

Clean the brass plates of a sizzler dish and heat up thoroughly. Cover them with cabbage leaves and arrange the cooked vegetables fast. Once again, place the dishes on fire and put butter under the cabbage leaves. The moment sizzling starts, place them quickly on their wooden trays and serve them sizzling hot.

The best accompaniments to this dish are any bread and soup.

Tips

Serving in a sizzler dish is just a style. If you do not own the sizzler plates, don't be panicky but serve the dish in a usual shallow serving bowl.

Variation

Instead of *Paneer*, use marinated and cooked chicken pieces or fish fried in small pieces and mix with the vegetables. Rest follow the same recipe.

Cooking time: 20 minutes for preparation and 25 minutes for cooking.

10. Paneer Squares in Hari Mirchi Gravy

Ingredients

(Serves 6-8 Persons)

For *Hari Mirchi* gravy

Almonds	20 gm
Cashew Nuts	50 gm
Cream	½ cup
Curds	½ cup
Lime Juice	1 tbsp
White Peppercorns	1 tsp
Black Cumin	½ tsp
Green Cardamom	4
Cloves	4
Butter	100 gm
Ginger Paste	1 tbsp
Bay Leaf	1

Water	2 cups
Coriander	A few sprigs
Green Chillies	100 gm
Sesame Seeds	3 tbsp
Red Chilli	2
Tamarind	A ball of lemon size
Jaggery (Grated)	A ball of lemon size (optional)
Asafoetida	A pinch

Tempering

Mustard Seeds	1 tsp
Curry Leaves	1 sprig
Oil	2 tbsp

Preparation for *Hari Mirchi* gravy

1. Soak cashew nuts in hot water for 15 minutes. Blanch almonds.

2. Grind almonds and cashew nuts with curd to a fine paste.
3. Pound cardamoms, cloves and pepper to a fine powder.
4. Chop chillies and coriander. Deseed red chillies.
5. Roast sesame seeds. Grate jaggery.
6. Soak tamarind in hot water for sometime and take out the pulp.
7. Grind together the green chillies and sesame seeds with a little water and coriander.

Cooking

1. Heat butter and crackle cumin in it. Add ginger paste and fry for a few seconds.
2. Add green chilli and sesame paste and fry for a minute.
3. Add almond and cashew paste, bay leaf, *asafoetida*, pounded spices, red chillies and salt. Fry till the fat oozes out.
4. Add 2 cups water, bring it to the boiling point and then simmer the gravy for 15 minutes.
5. Add tamarind pulp and jaggery. Cook for a few seconds.
6. Finally, put the lime juice and cream in the gravy and check the seasonings. Remove from fire.

Tempering

Heat 2 tbsp of oil for tempering, crackle mustard seeds in it and add curry leaves. Immediately pour the tempering over the gravy and cover it with a lid.

For *Paneer* squares, you require

Paneer	200 gm
Flour	½ cup
Thick Green *Chutney*	2 tbsp
Almonds	6

Cashew	6
Raisins	¼ cup
Cardamom Powder	¼ tsp
Pepper powder	1 tsp
Mawa (Grated)	¼ cup
Ginger	2-inch piece
Green chilli	2
Lemon	1
Salt	To taste
Oil	For frying

Preparation

1. Cut *Paneer* into 5 cms long and ½ cm thick slices. Gently rub them with the juice of 1 lemon and salt. Keep them aside.
2. Chop ginger and chillies very fine.
3. Clean raisins, wash and dry.
4. Chop almonds, cashew nuts and raisins very fine.
5. Mix together green chutney, chopped nuts, ginger, chillies, grated Mawa, salt, pepper and cardamom powder.
6. Mix flour with water and make a batter of coating consistency.
7. Take 1 slice of *Paneer* and place 1 tsp *Mawa* and nuts mixture on it and cover it with the other slice and press the edges. This way make as many stuffed squares as possible. If by chance, the *Paneer* is tough, mix it with corn flour, mash and make a dough. Take 2 small balls, flatten them with hands, place stuffing between the two flattened balls, press the sides and shape with hands.

Cooking

Heat oil for frying. Dip the stuffed squares in the batter of flour and fry on medium flame to golden yellow colour. Fry 1 piece only at a time. This way finish frying all the pieces. Place them on kitchen paper for some time.

Serving

Place the *Paneer* squares in a shallow dish and pour gravy around them. Reheat the gravy before use. Sprinkle chopped coriander, kept aside from *Hari Mirchi* ingredients, and serve the dish hot with any crisp *Roti/ Paratha* or bread of your choice.

Paneer squares can be served as a snack too.

Tips

The gravy can be cooked and stored under refrigeration and used when required. You may store it in small containers in deep freezer. It can last more than a week.

Variation

You can cook any vegetables, marinated *Paneer* or chicken, etc. with this gravy.

Cooking time: 30 minutes for preparation and 1 hour for cooking.

11. *Paneer Kadai*

Ingredients

	(Serves 4-6 Persons)
Paneer	500 gm
Ginger Paste	1 tbsp
Garlic Paste	2 tbsp
Chilli Paste	2 tbsp
Ginger	2-inch piece
Onion	2 small

Tomato	6 large
Green Chilli	6
Coriander Powder	2 tbsp
Red chilli Powder	1 tsp
Red Chilli	2
Kasoori Methi	1 tbsp
Coriander (Chopped)	¼ cup

Whole Spices

Cloves	6
Brown Cardamom	4
Cinnamon (Crushed)	1 tsp
Cumin	1 tsp
Salt	To taste
Oil for Cooking	¼ cup

Preparation

1. Cut *Paneer* into 1-inch square pieces.
2. Chop onions and green chillies. Cut ginger very fine.
3. Burn the skin of tomatoes. To achieve this, insert a knife or fork in a tomato and hold it directly on full flame, turn two/three times, slightly cool and peel off the skin. Now chop the tomatoes and keep aside.
4. Deseed the dry red chillies. Break them and remove the stem and seeds.

Cooking

1. Heat oil in a *Kadai*. Add the whole spices and crackle them.
2. Add chopped onions and red chillies. Sauté.
3. Add ginger and garlic pastes and coriander powder. Cook for a while.
4. Add chopped tomatoes, chillies and ginger.
5. Put salt and half of the chopped coriander. Mix, cover and cook for 5 minutes.

6. If required, add ½ cup water to the cooking *Masala*.
7. When oil separates, check the seasonings and add cubed *Paneer*. Mix it well. If the fresh cooked *masala* sticks to the bottom, add ¼ cup water and cover the *kadai* with a lid. Bring it to the boiling point, lower the heat and simmer the dish for 10 minutes.
8. Open the lid. Crush the *Kasoori Methi* leaves and sprinkle over *Paneer*. Cover with the lid once again and cook for 2 minutes. Remove from fire and serve.

Serving

Serve *Paneer Kadai* hot garnished with the remaining chopped coriander. The best accompaniment for this dish is *Tandoori Roti/Haath Lagi Roti* or fresh hot *Phulkas*.

This dish is supposed to be spicy-hot with the prominent flavour of fresh green *masala* and spices.

Tips

It is advised to buy commercially available *Paneer* for the dishes where *Paneer* pieces are one of the most prominent ingredients.

Variation

1. Use 500 gm boneless chicken instead of *Paneer* with the same recipe and cook *Chicken Kadai.*
2. Cook 100 gm each of green peas, cauliflower flowerets, halved mushroom, Baby corn and red or green diced capsicum with the same *masala* and you will have *Kadai Bhaji.*

Cooking time: 15 minutes for preparation and 30 minutes for cooking.

12. *Paneer Malabari*

Ingredients

	(Serves 4-6 Persons)
Onions	250 gm
Tomatoes	250 gm
Green Chillies	4
Ginger-garlic paste	2 tbsp
Poppy Seeds	3 tsp
Fresh Coconut	100 gm
Cumin	1 tsp
Cardamom	4
Brown Cardamom	1
Cinnamon	1-inch piece

Cloves	4
Red Chilli Powder	2 tsp
Turmeric	2 tsp
Curd	½ cup
Oil	¼ cup
Water	2 cups
Salt	To taste
Paneer	300 gm
Lime Juice	2 tbsp
White Pepper Powder	1 tsp
Cashew Nuts	12
Grapes/Raisins	1 cup/½ cup

(Hot and Spicy Preparation from Kerala)

Preparation

1. Soak poppy seeds. Wash and clean the grapes or raisins.

2. Peel and slice onions very thin.
3. Blanch tomatoes and pass through an electric grinder, strain and keep aside.
4. Take out seeds from the cardamoms.
5. Slice coconut and roast with cumin and cardamom seeds.
6. Chop chillies. Grind together chillies, poppy seeds, roasted coconut and spices with curds to a fine paste.
7. Cut *Paneer* into 1-inch cubes and marinate with lime juice, salt and pepper powder.

Cooking

1. Heat oil and fry cashew nuts, remove and keep aside for garnishing. In the same oil, add sliced onions and ginger-garlic paste. Fry till golden brown in colour.
2. Add pureed tomatoes, red chilli and turmeric powder, cinnamon and cloves. Fry well till oil oozes out.
3. When oil separates, add poppy seeds and coconut paste. Fry for 3 minutes. Add white pepper.
4. Add water and bring it to the boiling point. Lower the heat and simmer gravy for 20 minutes. At this point, add *Paneer* pieces and grapes/raisins to the gravy and simmer the dish for the time already mentioned above.
5. Adjust the seasonings and switch off the fire. Add the lime juice.

Serving

Pour *Paneer Malabari* in the serving dish and garnish it with fried cashew nuts. Serve it hot with either rice or *appams*.

- *Appams* are fermented rice pancakes and are very light to eat. They make an excellent accompaniment to any thick gravy vegetarian dish or non-vegetarian stew.

Tips

The northern part of Kerala state is called Malabar. Dishes of that part of the country are not only hot and spicy but also wholesome and simple.

Variation

1. You can add a variety of vegetables along with *Paneer* to this gravy and can cook *Malabari Vegetable Korma*. For this variation, cut vegetables and *Paneer* into small cubes. Boil all the vegetables before adding to the gravy.
2. Cook boneless mutton or chicken with this gravy.

Cooking time: 30 minutes for preparation and 30 minutes for cooking the dish.

13. Mock Eggs with Caldeen Gravy

Ingredients

(Serves 4-6 Persons)

For Mock Eggs

Paneer (Grated)	2 cups
Flour	¼ cup
White Pepper Powder	2 tsp
Turmeric	1 tsp (Levelled)

Salt	To taste
Oil	For frying

For Caldeen Gravy

Fresh Coconut	1
Cumin Seeds	1 tsp
Peppercorns	10
Coriander Seeds	2 tbsp
Turmeric	½ tsp
Onion	2 large
Tomato	1 large
Oil	2 tbsp
Green Chilli	2
Red Chilli (Whole)	1
Corn Flour	1 tbsp
Salt	To taste

Preparation

1. Grate coconut and mix it with cumin, peppercorns, coriander and turmeric.

   Grind to take out coconut milk. Take out first extract with 1 cup of water.

   Mix lukewarm water with ground coconut paste and churn once.

   Strain through a fine sieve. Again grind coconut roughage with 1 and ½ cup water, churn for 30 seconds and strain the second extract of coconut milk.

   Keep both the extracts separately.
2. Slice onion and chop green chillies.
3. Burn the skin of tomato by holding it directly on the flame.

   Remove the skin and chop it.
4. Deseed the red chilli.

5. Mix together grated *Paneer*, flour, salt and white pepper powder. Mash it well and divide it into 2 parts.
6. Take out one-fourth part and mix turmeric powder with this.

   Divide this yellow part into 8 portions. Same way divide the three-fourth white part of *Paneer* also in 8 portions.
7. Now take 1 portion of the white part of *Paneer* and roll it like an egg. Make a depression in the centre and place 1 yellow part to form the yolk of the egg. This way finish shaping all the 8 parts.

(From Goa)

Cooking

1. Heat oil for frying and fry one *Paneer* egg at a time.
2. Fry all the mock eggs on medium flame and place them on the kitchen paper. Keep them aside.

3. Heat oil for *Caldeen Gravy* and fry the sliced onions, chopped tomato and red chilli in it till the oil separates.
4. Add green chillies, salt, corn flour and second extract of coconut milk. Mix and simmer the gravy for 15 minutes.
5. Add first extract of coconut milk and switch off the fire. Avoid cooking after the addition of the first extract.

Serving

Take a shallow serving dish. Cut mock *Paneer* eggs into halves. Place them in the dish in a way that the cut-side is upwards. Pour *Caldeen Gravy* around them and serve. Aesthetically, white and yellow eggs surrounded with brownish red gravy look very appetizing. It's spiced coconut milk flavour makes it very special. Additional gravy can be served separately.

Tips

Though this modified Goan Gravy Caldeen is very simple to cook, yet a little carefulness is required after adding the first extract of coconut milk.

Always use boiled and cooled/lukewarm water to take out the extracts because no dish is cooked after the addition of the first extract of coconut milk.

Variation

Instead of mock eggs, you can put fried fish, boiled eggs or boneless marinated chicken pieces in the same gravy and cook.

Cooking time: 30 minutes for preparation and 30 minutes for cooking.

14. Paneer Peas Rolls with Nilgiri Gravy

(From South India)

Ingredients

(Serves 4-6 Persons)

For Rolls

Paneer	1 cup
Green Peas	1 cup
Urad Dal	¼ cup
Green Chilli Paste	1 tsp
Coriander Paste	1 tbsp
Ginger-garlic Paste	1 tbsp
Pepper Powder	1 tsp
Salt	To taste
Oil	For frying

Nilgiri Gravy

Fresh Coconut	1
Ginger	1-inch piece
Garlic	6 flakes
Cumin	1 tsp
Green Chillies	6
Coriander (Chopped)	2 cups
Green Cardamom	3
White Peppercorns	1 tsp
Cashew Nuts	15
Oil	1 tbsp
Water	1 cup
Cumin	1 tsp
Coriander Seeds	1 tbsp
Mustard Seeds	1 tsp
Pomegranate Seeds	1 tsp

Preparation

1. Roast *Urad Dal*, cool and grind it to a powder.
2. Boil green peas with a pinch of baking soda and mash immediately to a paste.

   It is easier to mash the vegetables when hot.
3. Mash together grated *Paneer*, green peas, *Urad Dal* powder, chilli, coriander and ginger-garlic paste.
4. Add salt and pepper too. Mash well and divide into 12 portions.

   Roll them in longish shape and keep aside.
5. Grate ½ coconut's white part only and grind it with 1 cup water. Strain and collect the first extract of coconut milk. Keep it aside. Slice the other half.
6. Soak cashew nuts in water for 30 minutes.
7. Roast pomegranate seeds/*Anardana* and pound.
8. Chop ginger and green chillies.

Paneer Kadai

Paneer squares with Hari Mirchi Gravy

Paneer Veg. sizzler

Paneer Malabari

Paneer peas rolls with Nilgiri Gravy

Mock Eggs with Kaldeen Gravy

Malai Kofta in Quick Gracy

Paneer Malabari

Amba Paneer

Palidaya

Paneer Melagora

Paneer Muttor Posto

Paneer Paratha

9. Now grind together sliced coconut, soaked cashew, ginger, garlic, green chillies, coriander seeds and leaves, cardamom and white peppercorns with ½ cup water to a fine paste.

Cooking

1. Heat oil to a smoking point, lower the heat and put 1 to 2 *Paneer*-peas rolls in it for frying. Fry them on medium flame. After each lot of frying, increase the heat for a while and then add the rolls. Place them on a kitchen paper for extra oil absorbance.
2. Heat oil and first crackle mustard and cumin in it, add curry leaves, salt and coconut paste. Sauté for 3 minutes.
3. Add 1 and ½ cup water and simmer it for 10 minutes but do not cover with the lid.
4. Add the first extract of coconut milk and pounded pomegranate seeds just before serving.

Serving

Take a shallow serving dish. First place the *Paneer*-peas rolls in this. Pour the coconut-coriander flavoured gravy around them gently and serve.

Paneer-peas rolls can be served as a snack or a starter on any occasion with tomato sauce or tomato *chutney*.

Variation

You can cook only *Paneer*, various vegetables and half worked mutton/chicken dishes with this unique gravy as *Kormas*.

Tips

Nilgiri gravy is unique in its nature, flavour and colour. We use coriander in various ways to make *Chutneys* and sauces and use it to garnish almost all the Indian dishes but this gravy is based on coriander paste.

A dish of green peas and *Urad Dal* powder or *Lobia* powder mixed with spices and fried in *ghee* was known as *Kattakarna* during the Vedic period. Here, we further mix *Paneer* with these ingredients and the dish has become very different in nature. Moreover, its serving with *Nilgiri* gravy makes it just yummy.

Cooking time: 35 minutes for preparation and 30 minutes for cooking.

15. *Paneer Kolhapuri*

Ingredients

	(Serves 4-6 Persons)
Paneer	300 gm
Onion	250 gm
Tomato	500 gm
Red Chilli (Whole)	10
Ginger-garlic Paste	3 tbsp
Coriander Seeds	2 tbsp
Goda Masala	1 tbsp
Turmeric	2 tsp
Mustard	1 tsp
Poppy Seeds	2 tbsp
Dry Coconut	5-inch square piece
Dagad phool	4
Nutmeg powder	A pinch
Cardamom	6
Cumin	2 tsp
Water	500 ml
Cooking Oil	¼ cup
Salt	To taste
Coriander (Chopped)	¼ cup

Preparation and Cooking

1. Peel and slice onions. Heat oil, fry sliced onions in it and grind.
2. Blanch tomatoes and puree.
3. Deseed red chillies. Slice dry coconut. Dry fry coconut, coriander seeds, *Daghad Phool*, cardamoms, cumin, poppy seeds and red chillies.

(From Maharashtra)

4. Grind them to a fine paste with the help of ½ cup water.
5. Reheat oil used for frying onions and crackle mustard in it.
6. Add ginger and garlic paste and fry till golden brown.
7. Add chilli, coconut and dry spices paste and fry on low heat.

8. When oil separates, add pureed tomatoes and fry further for a few minutes. Add brown onion paste at this stage and cook for 1 minute.
9. Add water, half of the chopped coriander and nutmeg. Simmer.
10. Meanwhile, cut *Paneer* into 1-inch long pieces and put in the simmering gravy and cook for 15 minutes. Add *Goda Masala* and remove.

Serving

Garnish it with the remaining chopped coriander and serve with *Rice Poli/Khakhra*.

Variation

Instead of *Paneer*, cook eggs, mutton, chicken, fish or any combination of vegetables with this gravy, for instance, cauliflower, carrots, peas, potatoes, capsicums, etc.

Tips

This preparation is a favourite of *Marathas* who prefer to eat spicy and chilli (hot) food. It is yummy for those who enjoy chilli or hot and spicy food.

If you can't eat chillies, omit the whole red chillies altogether from the recipe and instead use *Kashmiri* chilli powder which imparts only colour to the dish.

Cooking time: 30 minutes for preparation and 30 minutes for cooking.

16. Malai Koftas in Quick Gravy

(Gravy without Onions)

Ingredients

(Serves 4-6 Persons)

For Quick Gravy

Butter	100 gm
Tomato Puree	400 ml
Ginger Paste	1 tbsp
Cloves	6
Cumin	1 tsp
Cream	200 ml
Khoa/Mawa	25 gm
Red Chilli Powder	1 tbsp
Garam Masala	1 tbsp
Cashew Nuts	12
Coriander	A few sprigs

For Koftas

Paneer (Crumbled)	1 and ½ cup
Mawa	½ cup
Mixed Nut Powder	¼ cup
Corn Flour	2 tbsp
Basil *(Tej Patta)*	8 to 10 leaves
White Pepper	2 tsp
Salt	To taste
Oil	For frying

Preparation

1. Chop coriander and basil very fine.
2. Grate *Mawa* for gravy.
3. Mix together all the ingredients for *Koftas*, add chopped chillies and basil and divide the mixture into 12 to 16 portions. Roll them and keep aside.

Cooking

1. Heat oil for frying *Koftas*. Fry 2 to 3 *Koftas* at a time on medium fire. Remove and place them on kitchen paper.
2. Heat butter in a thick-bottomed pan. Fry cashew in it and remove.
3. Now crackle cumin in it and fry chopped coriander.
4. Add ginger paste and sauté it.
5. Put tomato puree, red chilli powder, *Garam Masala* and salt. Mix and boil till the gravy is thick and smooth.
6. Add cream and cook for 5 minutes on medium fire.
7. Finally, add grated *Mawa* and mix well. Cover it and keep aside for 10 minutes.

Serving

Take a shallow dish, place fried *Koftas* in it and pour gravy around them. Garnish with fried cashew nuts and serve hot with *Phulkas/Parathas/Naan* or steamed rice. You may serve *Malai Koftas* as starters.

Tips

You may fry *Koftas* in advance but put them in gravy just before serving.

Variation

Instead of *Koftas*, put 100 gm green peas, 100 gm halved mushroom and 200 gm cubed *Paneer* in Quick Gravy.

Cooking time: 20 minutes for gravy and 30 minutes for *the Koftas.*

17. Paneer Hara Chholia

Ingredients

(Serves 4-6 Persons)

For Punjabi Tari

Onion	200 gm
Tomato	300 gm
Ginger Paste	1 tsp
Garlic Paste	1 tsp
Cumin	1 tsp
Turmeric	1 tsp
Red Chilli Powder	1 tsp
Mixed Spice Powder	1 tsp
Coriander Powder	1 tsp
Chopped Coriander	2 tbsp
Cooking Oil	¼ cup

Paneer	200 gm
Green Gram	200 gm

(Paneer and Green Gram from Haryana)

Preparation

1. Peel and slice the onions.
2. Cut *Paneer* into ½-inch cubes.
3. Dice tomatoes and place them in an electric liquidizer.

Cooking

1. Heat oil and fry the sliced onions till golden brown. Remove and place with the tomatoes in the liquidizer. Grind and make onion-tomato paste.
2. In the same oil, add cumin and crackle it.
3. Add ginger and garlic pastes and cook till golden brown.

4. Add onion and tomato paste and fry.
5. Put turmeric, chilli and mixed spice powder. Cook till oil separates. Sprinkle a few drops of water if the *masala* sticks to the bottom of the cooking pan.
6. Add 3 cups water, mix and boil. After 3 minutes of boiling, reduce the heat and simmer *Punjabi Tari* for 15 to 20 minutes.
7. At this point, add green gram and *Paneer* pieces in the curry. Let them simmer with the gravy for 20 minutes. If the gram is not very tender, you may boil it or microwave it beforehand. Remove when gram is soft but not mash or touch it.

Serving

Serve *Paneer Hara Chholia* garnished with chopped coriander. Best accompaniment to this dish is hot roasted *Phulkas*, a favourite of the *Punjabis* all over India. You can serve it with plain boiled rice too.

Variation

1. In the same gravy, you can cook green peas and potatoes or peas and *Paneer*/mushroom-*Paneer* or many other combinations of vegetables or *Tariwala Murg*/*Tariwala Meat.*
2. To the same gravy, if you add 1 tbsp *Kashmiri Chilli powder/Degi Mirch* and replace *Garam Masala* with *Kashmiri Tikki Masala*, the gravy will turn into *Rogni Gravy* from Kashmir.

Tips

The masala of the *Punjabi Tari* can be prepared in advance and stored in smaller containers in the deep freezer according to the need of the family and the ingredients can be added to it later.

Cooking time: 15 minutes for preparation and 35 minutes for cooking.

18. Amba Paneer

(From Maharashtra)

Ingredients

	(Serves 4-6 Persons)
Mango Pulp	100 gm
Mango Fruit	1
Paneer	300 gm
Onion	1
Cashew Nuts	25
Ginger-garlic paste	2 tsp
Cumin	1 tsp
Red Chilli (Whole)	3
White Pepper Powder	2 tsp
Cardamom Powder	1 tsp
Mixed Spice Powder	1 tsp
Oil for Cooking	2 to 3 tbsp

Curd	¼ cup
Cream	¼ cup (optional)
Curry Leaves	1 sprig

Preparation

1. Soak cashew nuts in hot water for 30 minutes and grind with curd to a smooth paste.
2. Cut mango into pieces for garnishing.
3. Chop onion very fine.
4. Deseed the dry red chillies.

Cooking

1. Heat oil and crackle cumin in it.
2. Add red chillies whole.
3. Immediately add chopped onion and fry till golden brown in colour.
4. Add ginger-garlic paste and fry till light brown.
5. Add 2 cups of water, black pepper, mixed spice powder and salt. Boil for 5 minutes.
6. Put *Paneer* pieces in it. Cook for 5 minutes.
7. Add mango pulp, cashew paste and cardamom powder. Simmer for 10 minutes. Remove and check the seasonings.

Serving

Serve it hot garnished with mango pieces. Enjoy the dish with any *Pulao*, *Paratha* or *Rice Poli.*

Variation

With the same almond gravy and mangoes, you can cook chicken as well.

Tips

In Maharashtra, during the mango season, mango is eaten with almost everything, eg. with *Parathas*, *Poories*, *Pulaos*, etc. and people are very fond of mangoes.

The Indian food history gives the references that during the period of the great epic, "The Ramayana", many meat dishes were also cooked with ripe mango juice. Here, we have, innovatively, cooked *Paneer* with mangoes which turned out to be real delicious.

Cooking time: 10 minutes for preparation and 25 minutes for cooking.

19. *Paneer Melagora*

(A Dal Vegetable Dish from Karnataka)

Ingredients

	(Serves 4-6 Persons)
Tuvar Dal	½ cup
Spinach (Chopped)	1 cup

Fenugreek Leaves (Chopped)	1 cup
French Beans (Chopped)	½ cup
Paneer	200 gm
Grated Coconut	¼ cup
Milk/Coconut Milk	½ cup
Ghee	2 tbsp
Sesame Seeds	1 tbsp
Mustard Seeds	1 tsp
Ginger	2" piece
Tamarind	A lemon-sized ball
Jaggery	A marble-sized ball
Peppercorns	12
Cardamoms	4
Cumin	1 tsp
Salt	To taste
Red Chilli Powder	½ tsp (optional)
Oil	For frying *Paneer*

Preparation

1. Wash and soak the *dal*.
2. Soak jaggery in ½ cup water and tamarind in 1 cup hot water for some time. Take out thick tamarind pulp.
3. Pound coarsely the peppercorns, cardamoms and cumin.
4. Dry fry sesame seeds.
5. Cut *Paneer* into ½-inch squares.

Cooking

1. Boil the *dal* and sesame seeds with 500 ml water till the *dal* is soft.
2. Add washed and finely chopped spinach and fenugreek leaves. Reduce the heat and simmer the *dal* for 20 minutes. If required, add ½ a cup of water in it.

3. Heat oil and fry *Paneer* pieces in it. Immediately, put them in the *dal* mixture and let it simmer.
4. Heat 1 tbsp *ghee* and crackle pounded whole spices and pour into the *dal* mixture.
5. Put dissolved jaggery, tamarind pulp and salt also into the *dal*.
6. Now add the coconut gratings and further simmer the *dal*. If you find the *dal* thickening, add ½ a cup of water and check the seasonings. Simmer for about 5 minutes.
7. Finally, add thick milk or coconut milk to the simmering *dal* and remove from fire. Transfer the *dal*, *Paneer* and the vegetable mixture to the serving bowl.

Serving

Heat 1 tbsp *ghee*, crackle mustard in it, put asafoetida and chilli powder, and immediately pour over the *dal*. Cover it with the lid for 5 to 10 minutes and then serve it hot with plain boiled rice or *Phulkas*.

Variation

Along with *Paneer*, you can use vegetables like *Suran* /drumsticks/grapefruit/gourds/pumpkin, etc. You can even add fried thin strands of wheat dough. Use maximum of green vegetables.

Tips

Melagora finds mention in the books of yesteryears. We are told that it was a pleasure to eat various kinds of *Melagoras*. During those times, it was a dish of pulses and greens in which tamarind was eschewed and coconut gratings figured prominently.

The book of AD 1594 named **"The Lingapuran"** of **Gurulinga Desika** mentions that several vegetables can go into making the dish of *Melagora*. To make this dish, several *dals* like *Moong*, *Urad*, *Tuvar* or fresh

Chana Dals were first cooked with sesame seeds, then with the green vegetables, salt and coconut gratings and finally mixed with ghee, tempering and thick milk.

Cooking time: 30 minutes for preparation and 30 to 40 minutes for cooking.

20. Aaloo-Mutter-Paneer Posto

(From Bengal and Orissa)

Ingredients

	(Serves 4-6 Persons)
Paneer	300 gm
Potato	200 gm

Tomato	200 gm
Green Peas	100 gm
Poppy Seeds	50 gm
Coriander Seeds	2 tbsp
Cumin	1 tbsp
Red Chilli Paste	2 tbsp
Turmeric	1 tsp
Ginger Paste	1 tbsp
Oil	¼ cup
Salt	To taste
Coriander (Chopped)	2 tbsp

Preparation

1. Soak poppy seeds in warm water for 1 hour and grind with ½ cup water to a fine paste.
2. Peel and cut potatoes into ½-inch cubes. Put them in water to avoid discolouration.
3. Cut *Paneer* into ½-inch cubes and keep aside.
4. Roast coriander seeds and cumin; and with ¼ cup water, grind to a fine paste.
5. Cut tomatoes, place them in a blender and puree. Then strain.

Cooking

1. Boil peas and potatoes with a pinch of salt added to the boiling water.
2. Heat oil for frying *Paneer*. Fry cubed *Paneer* and place in water to keep it soft.
3. Heat ¼ cup oil, add ginger paste and fry for a few seconds. Add coriander and cumin paste, fry for a minute and add tomato puree, red chilli and poppy pastes, turmeric and salt. Fry till the *masala* is cooked and oil starts oozing out.
4. Add 3 cups of water, fried *Paneer*, boiled peas and potatoes. Simmer for about 15 to 20 minutes or till the gravy is half-dried. Remove from fire and check the seasonings.

Serving

Transfer this semi-dried mixed vegetables to a serving bowl, garnish with chopped coriander and serve it with steamed rice.

Tips

Oriyas also, like Bengalis, use *Paneer* mainly for making sweet meats and occasionally consume it as a dish. They use *posto* or *poppy* seeds (as they call it) for almost all the gravies, hence, vegetables cooked with poppy seeds paste are very popular in Orissa. Poppy seeds not only impart a flavour to a dish but also provide a body to the gravy.

Some good hotels and restaurants even regularly serve this dish made with *Paneer* for the vegetarian gourmets and is delicious.

Cooking time: 70 minutes for preparation and 25 minutes for cooking.

21. Palidhya

Ingredients

	(Serves 4-6 Persons)
Pumpkin	100 gm
Peas	100 gm
Paneer	200 gm
Pineapple	100 gm
Curd	300 ml
Ghee	1 tbsp
Maize Flour *(Makke ka Atta)*	1 tbsp
Turmeric	1 tsp
Ginger Powder	½ tsp

Mustard Seeds	1 tsp
Pepper Corns	10 nos.
Asafoetida	¼ tsp
Rock Salt	¼ cup
Curry Leaves	1 sprig
Salt	2 tsp

(A curd-based Paneer dish from Karnataka)

Preparation

1. Cut *Paneer*, pumpkin and pineapple into 1 cm small pieces.
2. Beat curd, maize flour and 2 cups water together.
3. Coarsely pound peppercorns.

Cooking

1. Boil 2 cups of water with salt and turmeric and put pumpkin, pineapple and peas in it. Cook till

the vegetables are soft and tender but do not over-cook it. Strain and keep aside.

2. Now put boiled vegetables in the curd mixture and cook on slow fire for 10 to 15 minutes. Add the *Paneer* pieces too in this mixture.
3. Add rock salt, ginger powder and peppercorns. Simmer the dish for 5 minutes and transfer it to the serving dish.

Tempering

Heat *ghee* in a ladle and first crackle mustard seeds in it, then add curry leaves and finally asafoetida. Pour the tempering on the prepared dish and stir it lightly.

Serving

Serve the dish hot with any rice preparation. *Palidhya* tastes very well even with crisp *Khakhras*.

Khakhras are very thin and crisp wheat *Rotis*, a favourite of the *Gujaratis* in India. These days they can be bought commercially as they are available in big food stores, all over India.

Tips

Palidhya was a class of spiced vegetables cooked in curd and finished with a tempering greatly in the ancient period too. Even today the dish is relished in the state of Karnataka.

Among the various food items cooked in Karnataka area mentioned in the book, *SHIVATATTVARATNAKARA* fit for a king, *Palidhya* is one of them. Hence, it is often called as a royal dish.

Cooking time: 20 minutes for preparation and 20 minutes for cooking.

22. *Paneer Yachchuti* (Shak-Kooti)

(From Goa)

Ingredients

	(Serves 4-6 Persons)
Paneer	250 gm
Peas	¼ cup
French Beans	10
Carrots	1
Cauliflower	1 small head
Red Pepper	1 small
Yellow Pepper	1 small
Tomato	1
Coconut	1
Onion	2
Red Chilli (Whole)	6

Cloves	4
Cumin	1 tsp
Cinnamon	½-inch stick
Coriander Seeds	1 tbsp
Peppercorns	10
Poppy Seeds	1 tbsp
Mace	1 tsp
Fennel	1 tsp
Nutmeg Powder	A pinch
Ginger-garlic Paste	1 tbsp
Star shaped *Anis*	1
Turmeric	1 tsp
Oil	¼ cup
Lime Juice	1 tbsp
Salt	To taste

Preparation

1. Grate and grind ½ a coconut with 1 cup water. Strain and take out the first extract of coconut milk; again grind it with 1 cup of water and take out the second extract. Keep both the extracts separately. Slice the other half of the coconut.
2. Slice onions.
3. Roast sliced coconut in 1 tbsp of oil, cool and grind.
4. Roast red chillies, coriander, cumin, fennel and mace. Add poppy seeds and keep on roasting until the poppy seeds are light brown in colour. Cool and grind everything to a fine paste.
5. Cut beans, cauliflower, peppercorns and carrots into 1 cm small pieces. Cut the *Paneer* also into 1 cm square pieces.
6. Partially boil the beans, cauliflower, carrots and green peas.
7. Burn the skin of a tomato, peel off and cut into small pieces.

Cooking

1. Heat 2 tbsp oil and sauté onion in it. Add ginger-garlic paste and stir it for a few seconds.
2. Put ground coconut, ground spices and sautéd onions in a blender. Add the second extract of coconut milk and blend all the ingredients to a fine paste.
3. Heat the remaining oil, put in the ground paste and cook for 3 minutes. Add 1 and ½ cup water, turmeric and salt. Simmer for 10 minutes.
4. Now put the *Paneer* pieces, boiled vegetables, chopped peppercorns and tomato in it. Cook for 10 minutes on slow fire. Sprinkle the nutmeg powder.
5. Add the first extract of coconut milk, stir and remove from the fire. Check the salt.

Serving

Add a dash of lime juice just before serving the dish. Serve it with *Pav* (buns) or Dinner Rolls.

Variation

Cook well-marinated boneless and half done mutton or chicken with this gravy or use your own imagination to create something new.

Tips

Yachchuti is the best example of a combination of east and west cuisine which originated several years ago. This Goan style gravy, in earlier days, was a farmers' dish who used to grow various vegetables and cook them in a special way with all these spices mentioned above, as 'Shak' means vegetables and 'Kooti' means cut into small pieces. But over a period, yachchuti has become a symbol of mutton and chicken dishes cooked in the Goan style.

Here the effort has been made to go back to originality. Hence, this preparation is so popular.

Cooking time: 30 minutes for preparation and 25 to 30 minutes for cooking.

23. Palak Paneer

Ingredients

	(Serves 4-6 Persons)
Spinach	2 bundles
Paneer	300 gm
Onion	2
Ginger Paste	1 tbsp
Garlic	8 flakes
Green Chilli	3

Pepper Powder	1 tsp
Cloves	6
Cumin	½ tsp
Milk	½ cup
Cream	¼ cup (optional)
Oil	3 tbsp
Baking Soda	A big pinch
Salt	To taste

Preparation

1. Clean, wash, chop and cook spinach with ½ a cup of water and a pinch of baking soda for about 10 minutes.
2. Rinse and squeeze the extra water. Puree the spinach with milk.
3. Chop onions, green chillies and garlic very fine.
4. Cut *Paneer* into ½-inch cubes.

Cooking

1. Heat oil, fry cloves and remove. Cool and pound to a fine powder.
2. In the same oil, crackle cumin and add the chopped onion, garlic and chillies. Fry till pinkish in colour.
3. Add spinach puree, pepper powder and salt. Stir.
4. Put the *Paneer* pieces in spinach and cook for 10 minutes on medium fire or till the water evaporates.
5. Add the cream and pounded clove powder, cook for 2 minutes and remove from fire. Save 1 tsp of cream for garnishing.

Serving

Garnish the dish with the remaining cream and serve. The best accompaniment to this dish is any crisp and roasted *Roti.*

Tips

Palak *Paneer* is a very popular hotel dish. To retain the green colour of spinach, a pinch of baking soda is added by the professionals while cooking it before being pureed. As a conscious housewife, if you like to avoid the use of baking soda, there is another way to retain the colour. After washing and chopping, when you cook the spinach, **do not cover it**. Cook for 10 minutes, rinse and squeeze. Store it under refrigeration in the deep freezer or the chill tray and use as and when required. Take out of the freezer, at least 1 hour before using it.

Variation

1. Instead of the *Paneer* pieces, use *Paneer* crumble and follow the same process.
2. Instead of spinach, use fenugreek leaves (*Methi*) with the *Paneer* crumble. Follow the same recipe but do not puree the *methi* leaves.

Cooking time: 25 minutes for preparation and 20 minutes for cooking.

24. Paneer Stuffed Baked Brinjal Canoes

Ingredients

	(Serves 4 Persons)
Brinjal (Large)	2
Paneer (Grated)	1 cup
Green Peas	1 cup
Spring Onion	3 with the green portions

Ginger	1 inch piece
Green Chillies	2
Chilli Paste	1 tsp
Tomatoes	2
Red Pepper	¼ of a pepper
Coriander (Chopped)	2 tbsp
Cumin	½ tsp
Pepper Powder	½ tsp
Mixed Spice Powder	½ tsp
Cooking Oil	3 tbsp
Cheese (Grated)	2 tbsp
Egg	1

Preparation

1. Chop the spring onions, green chillies and ginger very fine.
2. Burn the skin of the tomatoes and chop them fine.

3. Cut red pepper also into very small pieces. Save one strip for garnishing.
4. Cut the brinjals carefully into halves.

Cooking

1. Place a heavy-bottomed *tava*/griddle on fire and smear it with a little oil. Brush the cut sides of the brinjals with oil and place one by one in the centre of a hot griddle. Cook till the inside is softer. This way roast all the 4 pieces. Cool for 5 minutes and with a spoon take out the brinjal pulp without damaging the shells. Cut the pulp into very small pieces and keep aside.
2. Put the oven on moderate heat.
3. Heat the cooking oil in a pan and crackle cumin in it.
4. Add the chopped onions and green chillies. Fry till pinkish in colour.
5. Put in green peas, roasted brinjal pulp and ginger. Add 1 tsp of salt and cook till the pulp is soft and transparent.
6. Now add chopped tomatoes, red pepper and chilli paste. Cook for 2 minutes and then mix *Paneer* and all the spices. Cook till well blended. Remove from fire and adjust salt.
7. Sprinkle some chopped coriander. Break the egg in the mixture and mix well.
8. Stuff the brinjal shells with this mixture and sprinkle some grated cheese on the top.
9. Decorate with red pepper and bake in an hot oven for about 20 to 30 minutes.

Serving

Serve it hot with any Indian or Continental meal.

Variation

Do not add the brinjal pulp to the peas and *Paneer* mixture while cooking and also omit breaking the egg in it. Then, you will have a popular dish ***Mutter-Paneer Bhurji*** that can be enjoyed with plain *Paratha* or can be carried in the tiffin box.

Cooking time: 30 minutes for preparation, 10 minutes for cooking and 20 minutes for baking.

25. *Paneer Paratha*

Ingredients

(Serves 4-6 Persons)

Stuffing

Paneer (Grated)	2 cup
Mango Powder	1 tsp
Green Chillies	6
Ginger	2" piece
Coriander (Chopped)	¼ cup
Garam Masala	1 tsp
Red Chilli Powder	1 tsp (optional)
Salt	2 tsp

Chapati Dough

Wheat Flour	350 gm
Water	180 to 200 ml
Ajwain	1 tsp
Salt	1 tsp (optional)
Oil	For frying *Parathas*

Preparation

1. Sieve the flour and salt together. Add *Ajwain* and 1 tbsp oil. Mix half the water and start gathering the flour. Keep adding a little water time to time and knead flour to pliable dough. Cover it with a damp cloth and keep aside for 30 minutes minimum before use. Divide into 12 portions and keep covered.
2. Grate *Paneer* and ginger for stuffing *Parathas*.
3. Chop green chillies and mix with *Paneer*.
4. Add mango and red chilli powders, *Garam Masala*, salt and chopped coriander. Mix all the ingredients for stuffing nicely and divide into 12 portions.

Cooking

1. Heat a *tava* for *Parathas*.
2. Take one portion of the *Chapati* dough and flatten it with hands from the sides. Apply a little oil and place one portion stuffing in the centre of

the disc. Seal properly, dip it in dry wheat flour, press the sides of the stuffed ball with your hands and roll it with the rolling pin to 7 to 8 inches in diameter.

3. Place the rolled *Paratha* on the *tava* and cook. Turn the side and cook from the other side, too. Apply a little oil on both sides of the *Paratha* and cook till crisp. Repeat the process and make the rest of the *Parathas*. Either stack them in a hot case lined with a cloth napkin or keep serving them hot.

- If you do not eat fried *Parathas*, roast half done stuffed *Parathas* directly on the flame from both the sides and enjoy them hot with its accompaniments.

Serving

The best accompaniments to *Paneer Paratha* are plain curd, unsalted homemade butter and buttermilk.

Tips

Use one day old home-made *Paneer* to make the stuffing.

Use its whey to make the *Chapati* dough for softer *Parathas*.

Variation

Make *Makki-ki-Roti Paneer Wali* in a similar way. Knead the *Paneer* stuffing and maize flour together with the help of whey to soft dough. Adjust the salt and make *Rotis* on a fourfold cloth napkin sprinkled with dry maize flour. Shape them with your hands. Roast or fry the same way as the *Paneer Paratha* and enjoy with the same accompaniments.

Cooking time: 20 minutes for preparation and 40 minutes for cooking.

26. Ajwain-Flavoured Bhindi Paneer

Ingredients

	(Serves 4-6 Persons)
Paneer	300 gm
Ladies Fingers *(Bhindi)*	500 gm
Ajwain	1 tsp
Green Chilli Paste	1 tsp
Garlic (Chopped)	1 tbsp
Turmeric	1 tsp
Red Chilli Powder	1 tsp
Oil	½ cup
Salt	To taste
Coriander (Chopped)	2 tbsp

Preparation

1. Wash and clean the ladies fingers or *Bhindi.*
2. Remove their tops and cut them into small roundels.
3. Break *Paneer* into a crumble.

Cooking

1. Heat oil in a *Kadai* and crisp fry the ladies fingers in it.
2. Remove and place on the kitchen paper for extra oil absorbance.
3. In another pan, put 1 tbsp of oil and crackle *Ajwain* in it.
4. Add chopped garlic and fry till pinkish in colour. Put the green chilli paste and sauté for a few seconds.
5. Add salt, chilli and turmeric powder, and stir. Now mix the fried ladies fingers in it and mix it well.
6. Place the *Paneer* crumble in the same pan and mix gently. Cover the pan for 2 minutes and remove from fire.

Serving

Garnish the *Ajwain-flavoured Bhindi Paneer* with chopped coriander and serve hot with plain *Paratha.*

This preparation is ideal to be carried in the lunch box with *Parathas.*

Tips

Always wash the ladies fingers and clean them with a cloth napkin before cutting them into pieces.

Cooking time: 15 minutes for preparation and 20 minutes for cooking.

DESSERTS

1. Paneer-Strawberry Mousse

Ingredients

	(Serves 4-6 Persons)
Paneer	1 and ½ cup grated
Strawberries	12 nos.
Strawberry (Crushed)	½ cup heaped
Milk	½ cup
Gelatin	1 and ½ tsp

Note

It is important that all the ingredients in this recipe should be at room temperature. If *Paneer* and strawberries are stored under refrigeration, take them out at least two hours before use.

Preparation

1. Take a jelly mould, grease it, rinse out of water and place in the freezer compartment of the refrigerator to be chilled.
2. Chop 8 strawberries very fine and save the rest for garnishing and cut them into halves.
3. Dissolve gelatin. Mix it with 2 tablespoons water and keep it over the pan of hot water till all the crystals are dissolved. Keep it warm till used.
4. Put grated *Paneer*, strawberry crush and milk in a liquidizer and cream it. Add dissolved gelatin in it and churn it once again.
5. Take out the chilled bowl out of the freezer and pour the *Paneer*-strawberry contents in it.
6. Place the bowl in the freezer once again and keep it there at least for 30 minutes, otherwise it can be in the freezer for one hour. Remove it and place under refrigeration till used.
7. Unmould it before serving. For unmoulding, rub the sides of the strawberry mould with your hands, loosen the sides with a butter knife, tip the mould and cover it with a serving plate or a dish. Place the mould upside down and the *mousse* will slide in the dish.

Serving

You may decorate the prepared dish with halved strawberries or place one piece of strawberry each on the top of the individual portions while serving. Serve it cold.

You may set the contents in the individual ice-cream cups for the children. Follow the same process for setting it.

Variation

Use mango pulp and fresh mango pieces instead of strawberries and strawberry crush. Rest follow the same process.

Tips

By chilling the bowl beforehand, the setting time of the dish is reduced.

Homemade *Paneer* can be used for this preparation.

Cooking time: 15 minutes for preparation and 30 minutes for chilling the dish.

2. Mango Cheese Crepes

Ingredients

(Serves 6-8 Persons)

For Crepes

Flour/Maida	1 cup
Milk	1½ cup
Egg	1
Cooking Oil	1 tsp
Salt	½ tsp

For Stuffing

Paneer (Crumbled)	1 ½ cup
Ripe Mango	1
Sugar	¼ cup
Nutmeg Powder	A pinch
Almonds/Nuts	10 no

For Sauce

Mango Juice	300 ml
Corn Flour	1 tsp

Preparation

1. Sieve flour and salt together.

   Put in a vessel and make a depression in the centre.
2. Break egg in the centre and add milk. Mix with a beater till the batter is smooth and lump free. Pour 1 tsp oil over this and mix once again.
3. Cover and let the batter stand for 30 minutes.
4. Crumble *Paneer* and add the sugar and nutmeg powder.
5. Mix it well with your fingers till it is smooth enough to be handled.
6. Wash the mango and remove the skin. Cut it into very small pieces.

7. Now mix the mango pieces with the *Paneer* mixture.
8. Chop nuts very fine and mix with the stuffing.

Cooking

1. Heat a medium-sized non-stick pan or a seasoned tava.
2. Mix the batter once and pour one ladle (*Kadchi*) batter in a pan.
3. Tilt it till the batter spreads. Cook on medium fire and turn the side for a while.
4. Remove the pancake and keep it covered. Make all the pancakes for the crepes.

   Keep them warm so that they remain soft. This recipe will give you 12 pancakes.
5. Spread one pancake on the chopping board and place 1 tbsp stuffing in the centre.

   Spread it with a butter knife. If the edges of the pancakes are crisp, just trim them.
6. Now fold the pancake twice to form a triangle.
7. Finish stuffing all the pancakes and arrange them in a shallow ovenproof dish.
8. Heat the oven for moderate heat.
9. Put the mango juice in a pan and bring it to the boiling point.
10. Mix cornflour with 2 tbsp of water and pour it in the juice. Boil once and remove from fire.
11. Pour the sauce gently over the folded pancakes. Either place the dish in the hot oven for 15 minutes or cover it with a cling film and microwave it for 5 minutes.

Serving

Serve the dish hot. You may cool the dish under refrigeration and serve cold. Mango *Paneer* crepes taste great when cold too but one must try them hot. They are simply mouth-watering.

It is an ideal dessert for winters or for wet rainy days.

Tip

Pancakes can be prepared in advance, stuffed and kept arranged in a covered dish.

The juice can be added just before placing it in the oven.

Cooking time: 50 to 60 minutes.

3. Banana-Paneer Splendour

Ingredients

	(Serves 6-8 Persons)
Banana	2 to 3
Paneer (Crumbled)	1 cup
Jaggery (Grated)	¾ cup
Butter	1 tbsp
Almond Powder	3 tbsp
Cinnamon Powder	½ tsp
Milk	1 cup
Gelatin	1 tbsp
Water	¼ cup, if required

Preparation

1. Peel and cut the bananas into small pieces.
2. Mix gelatin with 3 tbsp of water and dissolve in the pan of hot water. Remove from fire and keep it warm in the pan of hot water.

3. Apply a little cooking oil inside a glass dish or a mould. Rinse with water without touching inside and place it in the deep freezer for chilling.

Cooking

1. Heat butter in a thick-bottomed pan and put the cut bananas in it. Cook till they are soft.
2. Add grated jaggery or brown sugar and keep stirring till the jaggery is melted.
3. Add the crumbled *Paneer* and cook for a while.
4. Add milk and stir well. Remove from fire and mix warm gelatin with the banana mixture. Pass through a liquidizer and mix the powdered almonds in it.
5. Pour the mixture in a chilled glass bowl/mould and place it once more in the deep freezer for 30 to 40 minutes. If you like, you may unmould it before serving.

Serving

Serve it cold. You may sprinkle the dish with additional almond powder.

Variation

Serve the Banana Splendour with hot Chocolate Sauce.

Tips

Never mix gelatin with cold contents. It should be mixed with the contents at room temperature. Home-made *Paneer* can be ideally used for this preparation.

Cooking time: 20 minutes for preparation and 30 minutes for chilling it.

4. Paneer Fried Sweet Rice

Ingredients

	(Serves 4-6 Persons)
Rice	1 cup
Paneer	(Crumble) 1 cup
Sugar	½ cup
Ghee/Butter	¼ cup
Beetroot	1
Green Cardamoms	6
Cloves	10
Almonds	10
Raisins	¼ cup
Pistachio Nuts	10

Preparation

1. Wash and soak rice for 10 minutes. Boil it along with cardamoms, drain and cool.
2. Boil beetroot or microwave it for 3 minutes. Remove its skin and grate it. Keep aside.
3. Blanch almonds. Sliver the almonds and pistachio nuts.
4. Wash and soak the raisins.

Cooking

1. Heat the *ghee* in a thick-bottomed pan or a *Kadai*.
2. Add cloves and crackle them.
3. Add rice and fry for 3 minutes on high flame.
4. Add sugar and stir constantly.
5. Add the crumbled *Paneer* and raisins. Mix these ingredients lightly but constantly and cover for about 2 minutes.

6. Uncover and add the grated beetroot. Stir constantly for about 2 minutes.
7. Remove from fire and add half the chopped nuts. Keep aside covered for 10 minutes.
8. Loosen the rice with a fork before serving.

Serving

Pile up the rice loosely in a flatter dish and garnish with the saved almond and pistachio nut slivers. Serve it as a sweet dish otherwise enjoy this preparation with plain curd.

Serve the prepared dish at room temperature.

Tips

- If you are cooking this dish for some festive occasion, decorate it with silver *vark* used for Indian sweets.
- You can use home-made *Paneer* for this preparation but *Paneer* should be made a day before use so that it does not have much water content in it.
- You can also boil the rice a day before and turn into this dish at a short notice.

Cooking time: 20 minutes for preparation and 30 minutes for cooking.

5. Rasogulla and Rasmalai

Ingredients

(Serves 6-8 Persons)

For Rasogullas

Cow's Milk	1000 ml

Sugar	2 tsp
Semolina (*Suji*)	1 tsp
Sugar for Syrup	2 cups
Water	1000 ml
Citric Acid Crystals	A pinch or
Whey from the previous lot	
Brown Cardamom Seeds	A few
Rose Water	(Optional)
Sugar Crystals	A few

Preparation and Cooking for Rasogullas

1. Boil milk, add whey and curdle it. Switch off the fire and let it stand for 45 minutes.

   To use citric acid crystals (*Tatri*), first dilute them with a little water and then add to the boiling milk. Rest follow the same instructions.

2. Drain the solids/*Paneer* and let it be in sieve for 10 minutes.

3. Place it in a flatter plate. Mash it well with your hands.
4. Add semolina and 2 tsp sugar. Mix and knead it well so that the dough is soft and fluffy.
5. Mix sugar crystals or bigger grained sugar well.
6. Make syrup with sugar and 1000 ml water and let it boil for 5 minutes; then keep it warm on low fire.
7. Now make marble-sized balls out of the *Paneer* dough.
8. Place one cardamom seed in the centre of each ball and roll it well.
9. Put the balls into hot syrup and let them boil on high flame for 20 to 30 minutes.

   Keep adding ½ cup water from time to time in the syrup to maintain the thinner consistency.
10. Cool the *Rasogullas* before serving. At this point, add the rose water, which is optional.

Serving

Serve them chilled.

- ***Rasmalai*** is a dish of flattened pattis of *Rasogulla* dough placed in thickened and flavoured milk.

For *Rasmalai* you require:

Milk	1000 ml
Sugar	¼ cup
Saffron	A few strands
Pistachio Nuts	2 tbsp

Preparation and Cooking for *Ras*, i.e., Thickened Milk

1. Soak saffron in 2-tablespoon of milk and keep aside.
2. Grate half the pistachio nuts and cut the rest into thin slivers.

3. Boil milk and thicken it. Reduce it to half the quantity.
4. Add sugar and boil once again. Switch off the fire.
5. Sprinkle the grated nuts and mix well.
6. Cool under refrigeration before serving.

For *Malai*, i.e., the solid part of the *Paneer*, follow the recipe of *Rasogulla.*

Instead of making marble-sized balls, flatten them and put in the boiling syrup.

Remove after 20 minutes and place them in the thickened milk.

Serving

Cool the *Rasmalai* properly before serving.

Garnish with pistachio nut slivers and serve.

Tips

For *Rasmalai*, you may have half the recipe of *Rasogulla* ingredients.

Rasogulla is one of the innovative sweetmeats made by the professional sweet makers. In 1868, the 22-year-old Nobin Chandra Das created the spongy *Rasogullas* cooked in sugar syrup and some 50 years later, his son Krishna Chandra Das invented the *Rasmalai*, flattened *Chhena* pattis floating in thickened milk. In 1930, he also started the mechanized production and canning of *Rasogulla* under the name **K.C. Das**, today popularly known as K.C. Das Rasogullas.

Cooking time: About 1 hour and 15 minutes.

6. Chhena Boondi with Rabri

Ingredients

(Serves 6-8 Persons)

For *Boondi*

Paneer (Crumble)	½ cup
Mawa	¼ cup
Flour	2 tbsp
Sugar	1 tsp
Baking Soda	¼ tsp
Sugar	1 cup
Water	1 and ½ cup
Green Cardamoms	4
Cooking Oil	For frying

For *Rabri*

Full Cream Milk	6 cups
Sugar	¼ cup
Cardamom Powder	½ tsp
Almonds/Cashew Nuts	12
Pistachio Nuts	10
Raisins	2 tbsp
Saffron	A few strands

Preparation

1. Mix *Paneer* and *Mawa* together. Add flour and 1 tsp sugar.
   Knead gently to resemble bread crumbs.
2. Mix baking soda with 1 tsp water and add to the *Paneer* mixture. Knead once again and keep aside.
3. Soak saffron in 2 tbsp milk.
4. Grate pistachio nuts and keep aside.
5. Wash and soak raisins, too.
6. Divide the dough into peanut-sized portions.

Cooking

1. Boil sugar and water for making syrup with cardamoms in it. Keep it warm.
2. On the other burner, keep milk for boiling to make the Rabri. Bring it to the boiling point and then let it simmer on slow fire.
3. Reduce it to one-third consistency, add sugar and cook on slow fire for a while.
4. Remove from fire and sprinkle cardamom powder.
5. Add soaked raisins and saffron too. Mix and keep aside.
6. Heat the *ghee* or oil in a frying pan to a smoking point and then reduce the heat.
7. Fry nuts and remove on kitchen paper. Cool and chop them.

8. Roll the *Paneer-Mawa* balls and deep fry them on medium flame.

   Keep stirring. Once pinkish in colour, remove on kitchen paper.

9. Immediately, place them in the hot sugar syrup. Boil on slow fire for 10 minutes and then gently remove from the syrup.

Serving

Arrange *Paneer Boondi* in a shallow dish and pour *Rabri* over it. Garnish with grated pistachio nuts and chopped fried almonds.

Serve lukewarm or cold according to your own preference and liking.

Tips

Home-made *Paneer* or *Chhena* can be used for the preparation of this dish but it should be drained well. *Paneer* should be made at least 2 hours before use.

Cooking time: 1 hour and 15 minutes.

7. Paneer and Sago Kheer

Ingredients

	(Serves 4-6 Persons)
Paneer (Crumble)	1 cup
Sago	½ cup
Milk	4 cups
Sugar	¼ cup
Green Cardamom	6
Saffron	A few strands
Almonds	6

Cashew Nuts	6
Pistachio Nuts	1 tbsp
Raisins	10
Melon Seeds	1 tbsp
Pure *Ghee*	1 tsp

Preparation

1. Wash and soak *Sago* in 1 cup of water for 15 minutes.
2. Roast almonds and cashew nuts. Cool and coarsely pound them.
3. Take out the seeds of cardamoms.
4. Wash and soak raisins.
5. Soak saffron in 2 tbsp of milk.
6. Sliver pistachio nuts.

Cooking

1. Bring 4 cups of milk to the boiling point, reduce the heat and simmer.
2. Boil soaked *Sago* with its own water and add 1 more cup of water for 5 minutes on full flame. Then mix it with the boiling milk.
3. Add cardamom seeds to the boiling milk.
4. Keep cooking for 15 minutes on medium fire.
5. Add crumbled *Paneer* and cook on low fire for 10 minutes. Keep stirring it.
6. Put sugar and cook for another 5 minutes.
7. Add pounded nuts and raisins too.
8. Remove from fire and pour in a serving dish.
9. Heat *ghee* in a ladle and crackle melon seeds. Pour over the *Sago Kheer*.

Serving

Garnish the dish with pistachio nut slivers and gently pour the soaked saffron in the centre of the dish. With a spoon, stir the centre of the *Sago Paneer Kheer*. Serve it lukewarm.

If you prefer to enjoy it cold, add ¼ cup or ½ cup milk before serving because the *Kheer* thickens when it is cold.

Tips

Sago first soaked and cooked in water for a while swells well and is good for this dish.

Cooking time: 15 minutes for preparation and 30 minutes for cooking.

8. Kshira Praka with Chocolate Sauce

(Sugar-coated Chhena Sweet)

Ingredients

	(Serves 4-6 Persons)
Paneer	250 gm
Rice Flour	¼ cup
Sugar	½ cup
Water	½ cup
Rose Water	2 tsp
Ghee/Oil	For frying

Chocolate Sauce

Cocoa Powder	¼ cup
Sugar	½ cup
Water	1 and ½ cup

Preparation

1. Crumble *Paneer* and mix it with rice flour. Knead it well.
2. Make fancy-shaped flat cakes resembling animals, birds and flowers, etc.

Cooking

1. Boil sugar and water together and make 1 and ½ to 2 strings consistency sugar syrup.
2. Add rose water and keep aside.
3. Heat thick-bottomed griddle or a pan, pour some *ghee* or oil and shallow fry fancy-shaped *Pattis.*
4. Just dip the Pattis in the sugar syrup, remove and place them on the wire rack so that the excess syrup drains well. Or, you may keep the wire rack in a tray, place the fried *Pattis* on top and pour the thick sugar syrup over them evenly to coat all the *Pattis.*
5. Let excess syrup be drained.
6. Cool the *Pattis* before serving.
7. Mix cocoa and sugar in a pan. Add 1 and ½ cup water and place on fire. Bring it to a boiling point, lower the heat and cook till the sauce achieves gloss and is of thick pouring consistency. Cool and store under refrigeration. The sauce lasts for more than 2 weeks.

Serving

Serve *Kshira Prakas* at room temperature with tea, with or without chocolate sauce.

Tips

Kshira Prakas make an excellent item for children's party. They find mention in the book titled ***The Manasollasa*** written in the 12th century by King Someshwara. It is written that *Chhena* was shaped like animals, flowers and birds, fried in *ghee* and coated with sugar. Even different geometrical shapes were given to this sweet.

Serving *Kshira Prakas* with chocolate sauce is modern innovation of this dish.

Cooking time: 30 minutes for preparation and 30 minutes for cooking.

9. Paneer Jalebi

(A Populat sweet dish of Bengal, Chhanar Jalebi)

Ingredients

	(Serves 4-6 Persons)
Paneer (Crumble)	1 cup
Mawa	¼ cup
Flour	¼ cup

Baking Soda	A pinch
Sugar	1 cup
Water	3 cups
Cardamom	3
Saffron	A few strands
Ghee/Oil	For frying

Preparation

1. Sieve together flour and baking soda.
2. Grate *Mawa*.
3. Mix together *Paneer* crumble, *Mawa* and sieved flour. Mash and knead it to soft dough. Divide it into lemon-sized portions.

Cooking

1. Boil together sugar and water in a *Kadai* or a pan and make a syrup of mild consistency. Keep it warm. Add cardamom seeds and saffron.
2. Heat *ghee* or oil for frying. Bring it to the smoking point and then lower the heat.
3. Take 1 portion of *Paneer* dough and roll it like a ½-inch thick bar/string and shape like a coil. Use a clean plastic sheet for this. Place the rolled bar on the sheet and shape. It will be easier to pick up the coil-shaped *Jalebis* from the plastic sheet. Shape all the *Paneer* portions like this and keep aside.
4. Now increase the heat under oil to medium and fry 1 hand-shaped *Jalebi* at a time to golden brown colour. Remove the fried one from the frying pan and place it in the sugar syrup. This way finish frying all the *Jalebis* and place them in hot sugar syrup.
5. Soak the *Jalebis* in the syrup for 30 minutes, then gently take out of it and serve. Add a little water if the syrup thickens because thick syrup will not make *Jalebis* soft and juicy.

Serving

Place the *Paneer* Jalebis in a shallow dish and serve at room temperature.

Tips

Since time immemorial, *Jalebi* is being made and described as a coiled tubular fried item soaked in sugar syrup. Essentially, it is a flat spiral fermented batter, fried and soaked in sugar syrup and then withdrawn. But the ingredients are varied, somewhere it is ground *Urad Dal* with a little rice flour as a binder is used and at other places gram flour and wheat flour which is generally very common. The batter is frequently fermented with curd. In Bengal, white flour, *Chhena* (*Paneer*) and *Mawa* (*Khoa*) are mixed to make *Jalebis* and then shaped by hand before frying and dipping in the sugar syrup.

Jalebi finds mention in the literature written almost five centuries ago. It is believed that the word *Jalebi* has been taken either from the Arabic word '*Zalabiya*' or from the Persian word, '*Zalibiya.*'

Cooking time: 15 minutes for preparation and 30 minutes for frying.

10. Orange Delight

Ingredients

	(Serves 4 Persons)
Orange Juice	400 ml
Gelatin	1 tbsp
Sugar	1 tbsp or
Orange Jelly	1 packet

Water	400 ml
Paneer (Grated)	1 cup
Oranges	2

Preparation and Cooking

1. Peel oranges and clean the segments.
2. Boil water and dissolve jelly crystals in it or mix sugar with orange juice and bring it to the boiling point. Dissolve gelatin in 3 tbsp water and add to it. Cool under refrigeration.
3. Put 100 ml jelly out of the prepared one or 100 ml juice in a blender. Mix *Paneer* and churn it for a while.
4. When jelly is half set, take it out and mix gently with the *Paneer* mixture. Transfer it to a serving dish and place under refrigeration. Take it out before serving and garnish with orange segments and 1 tbsp of grated *Paneer*.

Serving

Serve it cold. This preparation is very soothing, particularly in summer months.

Variation

You may use any other flavour of jelly like strawberry, raspberry or pineapple but follow the same procedure.

Cooking time: 20 minutes for preparation and cooking and 30 minutes for cooling it.

11. Sandesh from Bengal

Ingredients

	(Serves 4-6 Persons)
Paneer	250 gm
Sugar Powder	175 gm
Cardamom Powder	2 tsp
Rice Flour	2 tbsp, if required
Rose Water	A few drops (optional)

Preparation and Cooking

1. Grate or crumble *Paneer* and knead it well to a smooth paste.
2. Put it in a *Kadai* and add powdered sugar.
3. Mix and cook on slow fire to get it moisture free.
4. Cool and pass through an electric blender.
5. Sprinkle rose water and mix once again.
6. Use the roasted rice powder if your *Chhena* mixture is slightly wet.
7. Give any desired shape and apply a little cardamom powder on top of them.

Note

You can give impressions with the back of the fork or with the fork spikes.

Use moulds to shape *Sandesh*, if available.

Serving

Serve *Sandesh* at room temperature. If you like them cold, keep them covered under refrigeration and cool.

Variation

1. You can make two-coloured *Sandesh*. Add a few drops of edible colour in half the mixture, shape them and sandwich them.
2. You can add even chopped dry fruits to the *Sandesh* mixture.

Tips

Use fresh but dry *Paneer* for good results. If you are using home-made *Paneer* for this preparation, make *Paneer* a day earlier but keep it under refrigeration.

Sandesh is one of the most popular sweets of Bengal, which is made of sweetened *Chhena* and is cast in numerous moulds to resemble flowers, fruits, shells etc. It is given various colours and flavoured with cardamoms, rose water and orange peel, etc. It is believed that more than a hundred variations are prepared these days. This traditional Bengali sweet finds mention in the book ***Chaitanya Charitamrit*** written around the 16th century.

Cooking time: 15 minutes for preparation, 10 minutes for cooling the mixture and 20 minutes for shaping and decorating the *Sandesh.*

12. Chhanar Payesh

Ingredients

	(Serves 6-8 Persons)
Paneer	150 gm
Milk	1000 ml
Sugar	150 gm
Cashew Nuts	6
Almonds	6
Pistachio Nut	2 tbsp
Dates	6
Cardamom Powder	2 tsp levelled

Preparation

1. Blanch the almonds and cut into slivers.
2. Wash the dates and chop them fine.
3. Chop the cashew and pistachio nuts.
4. Cut the *Paneer* into small cubes.

Cooking

1. Boil milk and reduce it to half the quantity.
2. Add sugar and boil for 5 minutes more.
3. Put chopped dates into the milk.
4. Add the *Paneer* cubes to the milk and boil for 10 minutes.

(Bengali Style Chhena Kheer)

5. Remove from fire and sprinkle the dish with the chopped nuts.
6. Pour the *Payesh* or *kheer* gently into the serving dish.

Serving

Sprinkle a little cardamom powder on the *Chhenar Payesh* and serve it lukewarm.

Variation

Instead of sugar, you can use palm jaggery too.

Tips

Use fresh *Paneer* for this sweet dish. It is a very popular and famous sweet dish of Bengal prepared in festivals, marriages, etc.

Cooking time: Preparation time is just 10 minutes but the cooking time is 30 to 40 minutes.

Glossary

A list of commonly used terms for vegetables, fruits, herbs, grains, spices, seeds, pulses and names of a few preparations taken from various languages of India and translated in English.

Common Language - English

Aaloo — Potatoes

Aaloo-Bhukhara/Alucha — Plums

Aam/Amra — Mango

Adrak — Ginger

Ajwan — Carom Seeds

Akhrot — Walnuts

Amrud — Guava

Anaar — Pomegranate

Annanas — Pineapple

Angoor — Grapes

Amchur — Mango Powder

Amla — Gooseberry

Arbi — Colocosia

Arhar — Toor Dal

Baingan — Brinjal/Egg Plant

Badam — Almonds

Badi Ilaichi — Black Cardamoms

Baking Powder — Baking Powder

Besan — Bengal Gram Powder

Bhakri — Crisp Roti

Bhat — Rice preparation

Bhindi — Lady Fingers/Okra

Bhutta — Corn

Boondi — Deep-fried Droplets of pulse flour

Chai — Tea

Chapati — Flat griddle-roasted Wheat circlet

Chat — Combination of Food items, Chutneys and Spices

Chat Masala — Powdered Spices used for Chat

Chenna — Cottage Cheese (paneer)

Chironji — Chiroli

Cholia — Green Gram

Chote Aoloo — Baby Tomatoes

Chote Tamatar — Cherry Tomatoes

Common Language - English

Choti Ilaichi — Green Cardamoms

Chukander — Beetroot

Chutney — Spicy sauce of various combinations of food items ground together

Dahi — Curds

Dalchini — Cinnamon Sticks

Dalia — Broken Wheat used for Porridge

Desi Ghee — Clarified Butter

Dhania — Coriander Seeds

Doodh — Milk

Falooda — A drink made of Corn flour noodles added to sweetened and flavoured Milk

France Beans — French Beans

Gajar — Carrot

Ghee — Vanaspati Ghee

Ghenhu — Wheat

Gobi — Cauliflower

Gosht — Mutton/Meat

Gur/Guda — Coarse Brown Sugar

Haldi — Turmeric

Halwa — Semi solid Sweet Confection

Hara Badam — Fresh Green Almonds

Hara Channa — Green Gram

Hara Dhania — Coriander Leaves

Hara Pyaj — Spring Onions

Hari Mirchi — Green Chili

Hari Gobi — Broccoli

Hari Chutny — Ground paste of fresh Coriander and Mint leaves with green Chili and Ginger etc

Heeng — Asafoetida

Imli — Tamarind

Imli Chutny — Spicy sauce made of Tamarind pulp

Jaiphal — Nutmeg

Javiatri — Mace

Jeera — Cumin Seeds

Jilebi/Jalebi — Coiled tubular fried pastry soaked in sugar syrup

Kabab — Spit roasted pieces of Vegetables, Meats or Paneer

Kabuli Channa — Chic Peas

Kachori — Stuffed Flour patty

Kadi Patta — Curry Leaves

Kaju — Cashew Nuts

Kala Namak — Rock Salt

Kala Channa — Bengal Gram

Kali Mirch (Kali Miri) — Black Pepper

Karela — Bitter Gourd

Kas — Grated

Kela — Banana

Kesar — Saffron

Khajur — Dates

Khaskhas — Poppy seeds

Kheema — Minced Meat

Kheer — Milk and Rice Sweet Dish

Khichdi — Rice and Pulse dish

Kishmish — Raisins

Khoya/Mawa — Dry condensed Milk used for making Indian Sweets

Khumb — Mushrooms

Khumani/khurmani — Apricots

Kofta — Grated Vegetables or minced Meat, seasoned and mixed with a winding, steamed or deep fried and served with any gravy.

Kulfi — A frozen Confection, made of thickened Milk and set in metal Cones.

Lal Mirch — Red Chili

Lassi — Butter milk / A drink made of Curds

Lavang — Cloves

Lehsun — Garlic

Litchi — Litchi fruit

Machhi — Fish

Madhu/Shahad — Honey

Makhan — Butter

Makki — Maize

Malai — Fresh Cream

Maida — Refined Flour

Mattar — Green Peas

Maash/Urad — Black Gram

Masoor Dal — Lentils

Methi — Fenugreek

Methre — Fenugreek Seeds

Mirch — Pepper

Moong — Moong Dal

Moong Dhuli — Moong Split

Muli — Radish

Mungphali — Peanuts/Groundnuts

Munakka — Sultanas

Murgi — Chicken

Namak — Salt

Naan — Leavened Bread Baked in Tandoor

Nariyal — Coconut

Nashpati — Pears

Nimbu — Lemon

Palak — Spinach

Paneer — Cottage Cheese

Paneer ka Pani — Whey

Papad — Crisp sun-dried waffers

Papita — Papaya

Payesh — A Milk-Rice Dish

Phai — Fruits

Phulka/Roti — Dry Puffed Wheat Circlet

Pilav/Pulao — Meat or Vegetables Rice Dish

Pista — Pistachio Nuts

Pratha — Layered Roti fried on Griddle or roasted in Tandoor

Pua — Sweet Confection

Pudina — Mint Leaves

Puri — Crisp Deep Fried Wheat Snack

Pyaj — Onions

Rabbri — Clotted Cream Flakes

Common Language – English

Raie — Mustard Seeds

Rajma — kidney Beans

Rasa — An extract /Juice

Rava — Semolina

Safed Makhan — White Home-made Butter

Sag — Leafy vegetables or a dish made of them

Sarson — Mustard

Saunf — Fennel/Aniseed

Sev — Apple

Sepreta Doodh — Toned Milk

Sherbet — A cool Drink made of any Fruit juice or Rose flower

Sirka — Vinegar

Suji — Semolina

Sukha Meva — Dry Fruits

Soya Paneer — Toffu

Tamatar — Tomato

Tamater Pulp — Tomato Puree

Tandoor — An open Clay Oven

Tandoori — Any food cooked in Tandoor

Tarkari — Vegetables

Tatri — Citric Acid

Tejpatta — Bay leaf

Tel — Oil or cooking oil

Til — Sesame Seeds

Tulsi — Basil

Urad Dal — Black Gram

Varan — A dal dish made of Tuvar Dal

Wadian — Fermented and spiced Pulse-Vegetables lumps. Sun-dried, steamed/cooked with Dals and Vegetables

Zaffran — Kesar

Zarda — Sweet Rice preparation

Conversion Guide

1 tablespoon — 15 ml

1 tablespoon — 5 ml

a pinch — $^1/_8$ teaspoon

¼ cup — 60 ml (4 tablespoons)

$^1/_3$ cup — 80 ml (5½ tablespoons)

½ cup — 125 ml (8 tablespoons)

$^2/_3$ cup — 160 ml (10½ tablespoons)

$^3/_4$ cup — 175 ml (12 tablespoons)

1 cup — 250 ml (16 tablespoons)

1 level measure* of **Sugar Free** powder concentrate = 1 teaspoon of sugar

1 level measure of **Sugar Free** powder concentrate = 1 pellet of Sugar Free

References

1. *Indian Food, A Historical Companion* by Dr. K.T. Achaya.
2. *Vegetarian Gourmet Recipes* by Dr. Paul C. Bragg.
3. *Chinese Cooking* by H.K. Lee.
4. Photographs by Sanjay Jadav.

Indians are crazy about Chinese food. Since majority of the people love Chinese food, most of the restaurants serve it. Considering this craze the author has brought out her third book on Chinese food for you. In this book she has given you a great variety of Chinese dishes ranging from the hot favourites like fried rice, Manchurian, chilly chicken to the exotic like cloud swallows, steamed bao-tse, fragrant chicken, Chinese mixed grill to many other delightfully delicious dishes.

Get ready to enter the world of exotic Chinese culinary delights!

Demy Size • Price: Rs. 80/- • Pages: 112 • Postage: Rs. 15/-

Kabab has always taken the pride place on Indian cuisine. It has variety and class.

In this book, the author describes the simple process for preparing kababs from meat, chicken, fish, paneer vegetables, fruits etc. Several cooking methods of kababs have also been described including the dressing, roasting and presenting. It includes preparation in the tandoor, tawa, kadahi, handi, patila, over hot coals and in the oven, grill or microwaves.

Explained in easy-to-follow language to facilitate easy preparation, the book describes how both the vegetarians and non-vegetarians can enjoy and relish kabab—ranging from sweet to savoury or from spicy to fruity. Here for you is a distinctive selection of delicious kababs. Enjoy and pamper yourself with the culinary delights of kababs.

Demy Size • Price: Rs. 80/- • Pages: 136 • Postage: Rs. 15/-

Bake Fresh & Nutritious Continental Bread at Home

Are you sick and tired of eating breads from the market? Do you crave for fresh and nutritious loaf of bread taken out directly from the oven on your breakfast table? Then baking at home is a healthy idea. Whether you're apprehensively curious or an ambitious beginner, BREAD BONANZA will help you rise to the challenge of baking delicious breads that turn out every time. Continental breads can be made easily like the Indian flat breads.

BREAD BONANZA is the first of its kind in India that explains you from basics: every succinct description of the techniques with illustrations. Every lesson will clear your doubts and lead you further to master the most common types of bread: batter bread, egg bread, white bread, whole wheat bread, holiday sweet bread, flat bread, and coffee cake.

With BREAD BONANZA at your side, making bread will become fun instead of daunting.

This book's contemporary approach shows you the way to make homemade breads faster and easier than ever before.

Price: Rs. 125/- • Pages: 152 (Colour) • Postage: Rs. 20/-

'Foods can make or break you' is an established fact. That is why it is important to include the mushroom – one of nature's greatest wonder foods – in one's diet. Some varieties have anti-cholesterol and antibiotic properties. The common variety is full of high quality protein as well as B vitamins. With its irresistible taste, exotic flavour and rich aroma, the mushroom's delicious dishes are a healthy alternative to meat dishes. Keeping Indian tastes in mind, the author has innovated some easy-to-follow recipes.

The book contains recipes on starters, soups, salads and dishes for the main course. Some of the starters and quick stir-fried vegetable dishes of mushrooms are just ideal for tiffin boxes of children, working women and other office-goers. Most ingredients used are easily available. To retain natural taste and flavour, spices are used sparingly. Unlike some cookery books that are merely compilations, all the recipes presented here are tried, tested or innovated by the author and would be just ideal for daily meals. Besides, these dishes can easily be a part of any Indian or Continental menu set for special occasions too. In short, mushrooms used in everyday cooking will help maintain the good health of your loved ones.

Price: Rs. 96/- • Pages: 128 (Colour) • Postage: Rs. 15/-

A must for every housewife

Praises are showered on a gourmet who can churn out good dishes as well as present it well on the table.

The modern housewife is a very conscious lady and wants to move with the times. She wants to do her work better with the help of scientific equipments, technological ways and means, and give her work an artistic touch, thus saving her labour and time.

This book attempts to cater to not only the metropolitan housewives but also the small-town housewives. In order to acquaint them about how to organise parties, the etiquettes to be observed and the presentation of the food are all given for the benefit of the readers.

Apart from culinary delights from across the world, the book includes sections on:

❖ Ideal kitchen ❖ Art of serving and table decoration ❖ Table manners

Big Size • Price: Rs. 96/- • Pages: 144 • Postage: Rs. 20/-

Pamper yourself with the culinary delights

From the green valley and the gurgling streams of Kashmir down to the Malabar coast, the western ghats to the eastern horizon, India has a variety of culinary delights which are a treat to a gourmand's palate.

Indian Cuisine has been deeply influenced by the Mughals, Nizams, Portuguese, Dutch and the English who have enriched it and lent a unique aroma and flavour. The succulent *kababs,* the tongue-tickling taste of stuffed *paranthas, sarson ka saag, makki ki roti, khaman dhokla, farsan, puran poli, idli, dosa* and *sambar,* each lend a distinctive taste and rule the roost in most restaurants and hotels.

Indian Cuisine gives you a number of recipes from across the country which make the tongues drool with excitement. Both vegetarian and non-vegetarian delights are included along with a number of lip-smacking desserts.

Big Size • Price: Rs. 96/- • Pages: 104 • Postage: Rs. 20/-

With fast food and junk foods being the order of the day, thanks to our rushed modern existence, staying healthy is of prime importance. More often than not, we forego some of the most delicious food in order to stay healthy. It is not necessary to give up culinary delicacies to maintain good health. This book shows just how.

The author discloses dishes that are nutritious as well as low in calories and high on taste. This book takes readers on a journey of culinary experimentation with different recipes that can then be incorporated into a healthy lifestyle. The recipes are divided into four sections: Vegetable Dishes, Meat and Poultry Dishes, Seafood Dishes and Desserts. These calorie-counted recipes will help you maintain a diet that includes various types of food, ensuring all your nutritional requirements are met. So, eat well and stay slim and healthy with ***Over 100 Fat-free Recipes***.

Demy Size • Price: Rs. 80/- • Pages: 120 • Postage: Rs. 15/-

The ideal cookery book for beginners that goes beyond cooking

Cooking Made Easy is meant for beginners, particularly those who are clueless about cooking. It is also for people who are fed up of eating out all the time and for working bachelors who like to eat out everyday but can't afford to! Not to mention the smart working woman who is not yet smart in cooking.

Unlike other cookery books dealing only with recipes, this book also teaches the aspiring cooks how to identify the ingredients and recognise the importance of a pleasing presentation. It imparts tips on healthy habits. It also explains the significance of herbs, nuts and sprouts, which are healthy and nutritious. On the lighter side, readers are told about some funny food facts and interesting definitions and expressions on eating and cuisine. An exclusive chapter on microwave ovens dispels any lingering concerns the readers might have about their so-called harmful effects. Read this book once and food will never taste bland ever again!

Demy Size • Price: Rs. 80/- • Pages: 104 • Postage: Rs. 15/-